IN THE SHADOW OF THE DRAGON'S BACK

A Young American Girl in South Africa During the Early Years of Apartheid

GW00359977

RACHEL ODHNER LONGSTAFF

Culicidae
PRESS, LLC
culicidaepress.com

Ames | Gainesville | Lemgo | Rome

Culicidae Press, LLC
922 5th Street
Ames, IA 50010
USA
www.culicidaepress.com

editor@culicidaepress.com

Culicidae
PRESS, LLC
culicidaepress.com

Ames | Gainesville | Lemgo | Rome

For more information, please visit www.culicidaepress.com

Library of Congress Cataloging-in Publication-Data
IN THE SHADOW OF THE DRAGON'S BACK: A YOUNG AMERICAN GIRL IN SOUTH AFRICA DURING THE EARLY YEARS OF APARTHEID

     p. cm.
Includes bibliographical references
ISBN 978-1-68315-011-4
Longstaff, Rachel Odhner, 1944-
Apartheid–South Africa–Moral and ethical aspects
Children–Foreign countries–Attitudes
New Jerusalem Church–South Africa
Race discrimination–South Africa
Race relations–South Africa–Law and legislation–1948-1961
Durban (South Africa)–Description and travel
South Africa–Drakensberg Mountains–Description and travel
South Africa–Politics and Government–1948-1961
South Africa–Social Conditions–1948-1961

Cover design and interior layout © 2017 polytekton.com
Cover photo by Pehr Odhner. Kirstin on horseback facing the Dragon's Back, Drakensberg, Natal, 1954.

DEDICATION

*For all the girls and boys of South Africa who grew up
with me in the shadow of the dragon's back*

And for Naomi

Thank you

FOREWORD

Rachel Longstaff perfectly captures the innocence of childhood, of growing up in a peaceful, happy and supportive home set in a beautiful, sub-tropical environment. Her depictions of a childhood in a decade long past conjure up images of what life should be like, the kind of life many might wish they had experienced. And yet, at the edges of the security and serenity of her home, the darkness of Apartheid, the "Shadow of the Dragon's Back," was rapidly beginning to blot out the light—even though her understanding of what this shadow was, would take years to develop.

Apartheid was the "Dragon's Shadow," a dragon dedicated to devouring the people in its path to establish and maintain its power. No matter how carefully parents tried to shield their children from the shadowy tentacles, they could not completely hide the effects of the growing series of draconian laws underpinning the policies of white supremacy. Nor could they protect them from the results among the increasingly oppressed people around them, from the disparity between the white beneficiaries of the laws, and the black victims hidden in the dragon's shadow. The innocence of childhood insulates us from many of the realities of life, especially when there is a concerted effort to conceal them, but that protection is imperfect at best.

The author highlights the dragon's shadow as it fell, often unknown to her, on the idyll of childhood. The bald presentation of the laws enacted by the Nationalist government in the 1950s stands in stark contrast to the innocence of her childhood. The irony in the comparison lies in the Nationalists' thought that these laws existed precisely to preserve her lifestyle, to protect her. Instead they were a slow poison for that lifestyle, as for Rachel Longstaff and countless other young, white South Africans, innocence became tinged with fear, with a sense that something was not right. Eventually innocence becomes artificial, maintained at the expense of those black South Africans whose lives were destroyed to satisfy a governmental policy. And with this came a sense that the situation could not last, and a dread of how it was going to end.

Every dragon needs a St. George to slay it, a voice for the voiceless. It is a great relief, in reading descriptions of the various Apartheid laws—the shadow itself—to see flickers of light of those who stand opposed to Apartheid: the light of Nelson Mandela and his colleagues, the Black Sash, the English press, those who were banned for speaking out. At the time these voices were a weak opposition to the dragon, but the fact that they were there lent a long hope that eventually the dragon would be beaten back.

"In the Shadow of the Dragon's Back" deftly places these two realities side by side: the innocence of childhood and the creeping force of Apartheid, forces inimical to each other, existing in the same place at the same time. The result is compelling reading. As someone who grew up in the next decade, the 1960s when Apartheid was firmly entrenched, so many of the descriptions of childhood and its juxtaposition with Apartheid described in this book took me back to very similar experiences in my own childhood, to memories buried but not forgotten. South Africa has moved on from the Apartheid established in the 1950s, but the shadow remains in many places, reminding us that innocence lost is very hard to regain.

Andrew M.T. Dibb, M.Div., D.Th.
Dean, Bryn Athyn College of the New Church Theological School
Bryn Athyn, Pennsylvania

In memory of my brother,
Pehr Hemming Odhner (1933–1985),
who loved Africa

TABLE OF CONTENTS

Acknowledgements

I begin by thanking all the librarians from near and far who supported my research on the Acts of Apartheid. My daughter-in-law, Lesley Longstaff, Librarian, Fairfax Media, New Zealand, started me off by sending useful links, especially to the Australian newspaper collections in TROVE. She also sent me to the right people for permission requests. Thank you, Lesley.

Thanks to my friend and colleague, Dr. Doris Van Kampen-Breit, Faculty Development Librarian at the Daniel Cannon Memorial Library, Saint Leo University. Doris supplied me with multiple links and ideas. Doris, you have been a supportive presence throughout the process. Many thanks also to Carol Ann Moon, Reference and Instructional Outreach Librarian, and Renee Gould, Technical Services Supervisor, both at Saint Leo University.

Many thanks to Dr. Daniel Reboussin, African Studies Curator, Department of Special and Area Studies Collections, at the George A. Smathers Library, University of Florida, Gainesville, who introduced me to the Gwendolen M. Carter Collection at the University of Florida.

Dr. Archie Dick, Professor of Information Science at the University of Pretoria, thank you for informing me about *Digital Innovation South Africa*. I contacted Dr. Dick, a prolific author, about an article he wrote on the role of the courageous librarians who supplied prisoners with reading material in apartheid South Africa.

Many thanks to Denise Nicholson, Scholarly Communications Librarian at Witwatersrand University, Johannesburg, for essential information about the South African Copyright Law. Others in South Africa include the South African History Archives intern, Kerry-Lee Clark, who gave me permission to quote *Women Hold up Half the Sky*, from an exhibit mounted in memory of the 1956 Women's March.

I am indebted to Victoria Rowan, Creative Consultant, Ideasmyth.com for many weeks of patiently pointing out that I could improve my writing if I would just start from the beginning and describe my characters. Her suggestion that I write my story as a series of vignettes, rather than in a chronological style, changed my whole vision of this memoir.

I especially wish to thank my niece, Naomi Pitcairn, artist, activist, and street artist extraordinaire, for her generous help and encouragement, and friendly commiseration. Naomi, your unwavering support for my efforts means a lot to me, especially as you were, at the same time, actively taking part in important causes around the country. And thanks for putting all these photos into 300 dpi.

To my brothers and sisters, both late and present, there aren't enough words to describe how grateful I am for your help, your stories, your photographs, your love, and your belief in me. Thank you, Pehr, Kirstin, Jeannette, Michael, and Siri. Special thanks, Mike, for your invaluable help with the photographs: you have done a great job with them—labels, dates, and all. Humble thanks, also, to our parents, Beryl and Philip Odhner, for giving us such an amazing childhood in spite of all the hurdles they had to overcome.

I cannot complete this list of supporters without mentioning my loving husband, Alan. Thank you for cooking and cleaning and lifting heavy pots when I got wrist tendonitis as a result of spending too much time working with a mouse at the computer; and for your patience in listening to me go on and on about the horrors of apartheid, I thank you. Our four children, Sarah, Michael, Stephanie, and Jonathan (and nine grandchildren) have also followed along and supported me in this adventure. Thank you all.

Finally, thanks to my editor at Culicidae Press, Mikesch Muecke, and his peer review readers, for believing in my story and for encouraging me to expand the content to illustrate how apartheid affected the people who lived under its burden. Thank you.

Rachel Longstaff

LIST OF ILLUSTRATIONS

All photographs taken by Pehr Odhner
unless otherwise noted.

Dedication
Pehr Hemming Odhner, 1933–1985

Introduction
Frontispiece. Robert C. Triggs. Family portrait, back: Kirstin, Jeannette, Pehr, Michael, front-row: Siri, Mother, Dad, Rachel, Durban, South Africa, 1954

Prologue
Passport photo U.S. Passport service, New York, 1948
306 Vause Road. House where we first stayed in Durban, 1948

Chapter 1 185 Sydenham Road
185 Sydenham Road at time of purchase. View from back, showing church. Durban, 1949.
185 Sydenham Road prior to moving in, front view. Durban, 1949.
Rachel and Siri on swing, Jeannette at right. Durban, 1950
Kirstin and Jeannette at new house. Durban, 1949
Jeannette and Michael on 3rd-floor balcony looking toward Durban Bay. Durban, 1950
Rachel playing the piano in the church, Durban, 1958
Sophie and Nellie, Siri's nannies, 1950
Garage before being converted to study. Durban, 1949
Tennis court prior to renovation. Durban, 1949
Family at dinner table, Durban, 1951 (note brass Mizrach plate on mantel)
Margaret Mary, Siri and Jeannette by Meg's car, 1957
Music room used as Church. Michael, 1956
South African Government issued identity card, Michael Odhner, 1958

14

Chapter 3 No Eulogy for a Black Man
Kirstin and Jeannette at front door (note leaded glass window in door)

Chapter 5 Market Day
Rachel and Michael shelling peas. Vause Road, Durban, 1949
Making ice cream using hailstones. Alpha Farm, 1951
Group exploring a Bushman cave near Alpha Farm. Ladybrand, Free
    State, 1951
Mother's market basket

Chapter 6 The African Ministers
Dad's study after renovation. Durban, 1950
Siri with Dad's safe full of Swedenborg first editions, 1955
Mayville Hostel, 1951
Rev. Benjamin Ngiba. Durban, 1959
Rev. Paul Buthelezi's house. Hambrook, KwaZulu, Natal, 1990
Pehr on horseback in the Maluti Mountains of Lesotho. Sequnyane,
    1961 (photographer unknown)
Church group in Lesotho, Mother and Dad in center, 1939 (photog-
    rapher unknown)
Rev. Gershon Mphatse and Mrs. Evodia Mphatse with school at Kho-
    pane, Lesotho, 1959
Jeannette on swing, 1956 (door to Billy's office in back)
African ministers with family at Farewell gathering. Mayville, 1960

Chapter 7 Our Friend Victor
Miriam Nyandu, our cook, Victor's grandmother. Durban, 1954
Group on front lawn. Durban, 1953

Chapter 8 Piet
Jeannette and Rachel leaving for school. Piet in background, sweeping
    front porch. Note leaded glass in front door. 1954

Chapter 9 Tennis Whites
Tennis court after renovation. View from 3rd-floor balcony. Durban, 1950
Siri dressed in tennis whites. Durban, 1958

Chapter 14 The Quality of Night

The Starry Heavens. Drawing for Christmas card by Beryl C. Odhner, 1965

Chapter 15 A Quick Trip to America

U.S. Consular Service, Passport Photo, Durban, 1956

African ministers at the Durban docks to wish us Bon Voyage, Durban, 1956

Dad and young men on ship, Atlantic Ocean, 1925 (photographer unknown)

Chapter 16 School Days

Rachel in Durban Girls College uniform, 1952

Chapter 19 Climbing with My Brother

The Drakensberg, "mountains of the dragon," 1952

Pehr's canvas knapsack and walking stick, Drakensberg, Natal, 1952

INTRODUCTION

Reaching into the past means nothing if it does not change the present[1]
Nancy Napier

Why do mountains inspire equally the artist, the poet, and the nature-lover? They are beautiful, but there is something else—a feeling of power, ancient, and forbidding. Mountains can be many millions of years old, like the Drakensberg, the "dragon mountains" of South Africa. The Zulu call them *uKhalamba*, "barrier of spears," so named for their jagged, serrated, stone cliffs. Tolkien's Merry worried about what lay beyond the mountains of Rohan, in the land of MiddleEarth.[2] I wondered what was hiding in the shadow of the Dragon's Back.

Time transforms memory. Like a painting, it is sensitive to change and exposure, and the natural aging process. My younger daughter has explained my eccentricities by saying, "it's because she grew up in South Africa." It has always saddened me that I have not been able to share with my husband and children what was an exotic childhood in a faraway country more than a half century in the past. I am sure my daughter is partially correct in her assessment: attitudes and opinions are inescapably and unintentionally formed in the context of culture, where the day-to-day business of living may seem similar in structure to what she knows and yet, at the same time, so foreign, even as to its very flavor and smell.

After several attempts to write about apartheid, researching history and politics, I discovered that my real purpose in writing was buried in the need to come to terms with the feelings that have haunted me since as a young adult I learned the truth about that history—a significant turning point in my life. As I worked, these stories kept slipping past the gates of my conscience, demanding attention, influencing the direction of my writing, so I chose to offer the reader a glimpse into the life of a young white American girl growing up in South Africa in the 1950s. The book is not intended to be a political commentary. Instead, the stories are focused on everyday life in a unique place and time in history.

Presented as a group of verbal snapshots, supported by the photographs my brother took for our grandparents in America, I hoped to transcend the limitations of a child's memory and subtly reflect the parallel world that existed in the shadows. The pictures portray a happy, interesting life, but a story woven through with dark threads of ignorance of the political holocaust that was apartheid. I have described my becoming aware of apartheid as being like mold growing on an oriental carpet. It was beautiful, wasn't it ... once upon a time? There is also evidence of a different kind of discrimination found in the culture of a British colony.

"I had a farm in Africa," the immortal words of Isak Dinesen, Baroness Blixen, so beautifully intoned by Meryl Streep at the start of the film, *Out of Africa,* came to mind as I began to write this introduction. Could six simple words so perfectly sum up the experience I am attempting to capture with these stories? I could say, quite simply, "I grew up in Africa," perhaps, but it wouldn't expose the painful dichotomy, the inescapable contradictions: the happy, sunny, colonial-style childhood contrasted to the harsh, dark, and difficult lives of those who lived under the laws of apartheid. To provide that contrast and put the stories in context, I have separated the chapters with examples of the Acts of Apartheid legislation. To me they are like a church bell tolling, announcing a death.

1954 Durban

Frontispiece. Robert C. Triggs. Family portrait, back: Kirstin, Jeannette, Pehr, Michael, front-row: Siri, Mother, Dad, Rachel, Durban, South Africa, 1954

I chose the title long before I started writing. The very words, "In the Shadow of the Dragon's Back," embody for me the story that I need to tell. Some of our favorite family memories are centered on the little thatched-roof house my brother built for us in the foothills of the Drakensberg, an area of compelling, wild beauty. When early Dutch pioneers first saw the Drakensberg, they must have felt the awesome power in those ancient basalt peaks for they named them the "mountains of the dragon." Because of its rugged, steeply leaning shape, one of the mountains is called *The Dragon's Back*. All of us, the children of South Africa at that time, black, white, or mixed race, grew up in its shadow, the dark energy of apartheid.

The realization that I did not personally earn my guilt has led to a place where I could confront that once hidden reality, give it some kind of form, and then let it go. It has left me with the freedom to hollow out a comfortable space where my stories can remain just what they are, stories from another time and place, stories brought from far away.

Racism has certainly not disappeared from South Africa, and in the United States and elsewhere insensitivity towards minorities is escalating. Differences in politics, ethnicity, and religion have disrupted cities and towns and moved thousands of men, women, and children to risk all they have to reach safety and freedom.

PROLOGUE

My father, Philip Odhner, was a Swedenborgian minister, following the faith of his grandparents and great-grandparents for several generations, as did his own father—a feisty Swedish immigrant whose older brother handed him a one-way ticket to America in 1882 because he was becoming too outspoken politically. Dad's mother was a beautiful woman of Greek and English descent whose own mother marched with Susan B. Anthony, the suffragette, and who was subsequently disowned by her well-to-do family. My father was one of the youngest of their thirteen children, orphaned as a young boy when both his parents died within a few years of each other. Having served as a minister in South Africa prior to World War II, he was now charged with setting up a theological school for African ministers. The large numbers of African members of the church were interested in having their own priests in an effort to rise above the status of church mission, so our father was asked to move the family to South Africa to serve their educational needs. He initially set up his classroom in the converted garage of a big, old Victorian mansion.

He also served as pastor to the European, or "white," church members in the city of Durban. I believe that it took courage on my parents' part to remain dedicated to their calling in that uncertain and increasingly complicated environment. Children observe and reflect the behavior of the people around them. I have spent a lot of time reflecting on my parents' need to shelter us from things they believed children did not need to know, perhaps what they themselves did not fully understand. There were many things we were unaware of because we couldn't or didn't ask. At home and at school we were taught not to question authority: "because that's the way it is." To step out of line would invite unwelcome scrutiny. The result is that the child interprets something seen or heard in a way that may or may not be true. I was left with a creeping malaise and a long-lasting fear of the dark that has haunted me for many years. *"It isn't fear of the dark, per se … It's the fear of what the dark conceals.*[3]

Born out of a feeling that I was somehow to blame for enjoying a happy, sunny childhood while others living in the same time and place were suffering, I have reached into my past to find these uneven parallels. I began by writing about apartheid, the racist system of segregation imposed on black Africans by their government, but this path proved thorny, obstructed by too many unanswered questions. Not only was I just a child at the time, but many more knowledgeable men and women have written about the life and politics of South Africa from a variety of perspectives.

When people ask me about my slightly unusual accent, I am inclined to tell them that I grew up in Africa. If they ask which country, I tell them, truthfully, and say, "It's a beautiful country," and hope they leave it there and won't ask me about the country's politics. I have many happy memories of swimming in the ocean and spending vacations in the Drakensberg, but these images conflict with the uncomfortable reality of the black South Africans who also lived through those years.

For some time I had wanted to do the work it would take to uncover the feelings that took hold in my mind, so after retiring from my job as a librarian, I asked my siblings to share some of their memories with me. As you would expect, the older siblings remembered more than the younger ones. Sadly, the two oldest, our brother Pehr and sister Kirstin, have passed away, as have our parents. We truly miss their insight. Because email quickly became too cumbersome, I created a social media site where we could post and comment on each other's stories. As we traded memories, my brother Michael discovered he had a set of negatives for the photographs Pehr had taken when we lived in South Africa. Pehr loved photography. He took hundreds of photos from the time we first arrived in Durban, developed them himself, and carefully identified the subjects, noting names, locations, and dates. Copies of the photos were sent to our grandparents in America. He started out with a Brownie box camera, but progressed to a Zeiss Ikoflex twin lens camera which he could manually focus. In addition to the neatly cataloged negatives, Pehr kept the manual for his camera, too. His photo album has disappeared but, fortunately, Mike inherited the negatives. The photos provide a chronicle of our lives from the beginning of our adventure in 1948 until 1960, when most of us returned to America. With the help of Pehr's photos, our story has come alive: it's the story of a family.

Odhner Family. Pehr, Kirstin, Jeannette ...
U.S. Passport Service, New York, 1948

We were a family of eight: six children, the youngest being Siri, an infant of four months, and the oldest, Pehr, was fourteen years old when we left New York City and crossed the Atlantic on a Pan American propeller plane. I was just three years old. Dad said he counted the six children and the twenty-five suitcases over and over again, to make certain they were all there. The journey took three days, considerably less time than a weeks-long shipboard crossing, but it was not without its trials, starting with our delayed departure from New York when the steward and stewardess were arrested for diamond smuggling.

House on Vause Road where we first lived, Durban, South Africa, 1948

Each stop in the long flight was for the purpose of refueling. Flying from New York to Gander, Newfoundland, we crossed the Atlantic Ocean to Lisbon, then proceeded down along the west coast of Africa to Accra; Leopoldville (now Kinshasa); Johannesburg, and Durban. It was nine thousand miles, plus a return trip to Accra to wait for a new engine when one of ours failed in flight. We reached Durban at last, a beautiful east coast port on the Indian Ocean, where we were to live for the next twelve years. Our Mother had packed up a home, moved to temporary lodgings, delivered a baby, and said goodbye to her elderly parents, all before she set off for Africa. It is perhaps not surprising that she was admitted to the hospital with pneumonia immediately upon arrival, leaving our Dad and our oldest sister Kirstin, who was only twelve, to take care of the rest of us, including the baby, while we settled into a new home in a strange country.

The Afrikaner government distrusted American missionaries—over the years the churches had built schools and educated the blacks. The government feared a middle class of educated blacks. In fact, several leading African political activists, Albert Luthuli, Walter Sisulu, and Nelson Mandela, were educated in mission schools. We were not missionaries, a term that makes me defensive when discussing my background. I don't mean to imply that there is anything wrong with missionaries, but my father's job was to establish a theological school. He was not stationed "out in the bush" like the missionary in the movie, *The African Queen,* which is what many people picture when you tell them your father was a minister in South Africa. Durban was a good-sized city of about a half million people in the 1950s.

As the years went by and the apartheid government became more entrenched, my father was required to register a constitution with the national government in Pretoria. In order to stay and provide theological schooling in South Africa he was told he must spell out exactly what the church was doing in South Africa, how it was governed, and list its basic teachings. All this was to be provided in four languages: English, Afrikaans, Zulu, and Sotho. Dad or Pehr drove back and forth several times between Durban and Pretoria—a distance of over three hundred miles—before the wording of the document was finally accepted by the officials.

Consequently, my father has said he felt that everything he did was with one hand tied behind his back. He couldn't criticize the policy of racial separation or refuse to comply with the law, for then the church would be closed down, and we would be deported.

But what is there to write about if not the history of apartheid? In whatever way I approached my task, it was the little stories of family life that finally inspired my writing: stories about sandy feet, muddy roads, mountain fires, panama hats, and the cry of a hyena, all covered over with the fresh clean scents of dry veld grass and sun-warmed granadilla fruit.

Chapter 1

The House Where We Lived: 185 Sydenham Road

One of Durban's oldest properties, at the corner of Sydenham and Musgrave Roads, has been bought for £8,000 by The Lord's New Church, Nova Hierosolyma (New Jerusalem). The property includes a hall, which will be dedicated as a church this morning by the Rev. Philip N. Odhner.

The house was built by one of Natal's earliest settlers, Mr. T.W. Edmonds, about 70 years ago. It is still in good condition and will be used as a manse. It stands on three-quarters of an acre.

The Sunday Tribune, Durban, 1949

185 Sydenham Road at time of purchase. View from back, showing church, Durban, South Africa, 1949

Shabby and old-fashioned, nearly one hundred years old, the house on Sydenham Road only just managed to hold on to its air of Victorian elegance. It was a wonderful place for a child to grow up. Graced in the front by a broad tiled terrace, it boasted tall white pillars and a red-tiled roof. High ceilings, deep verandas, and big windows kept the house cool and filtered the evening breezes from the Indian Ocean. From the little balconies on the third floor we could see the city and Durban Bay spread out in front of us all the way to the sea. When we first arrived in Durban, we had lived in a house that was much too small, but this big house was perfect for us.

Front view of 185 Sydenham Road, prior to moving in, 1949

On the street side the house was shaded by big old mango trees just begging to be climbed. Our father hung two swings from the branches. He made sure that one of them was low enough for the youngest ones in the family. Siri's nanny, Nellie, counted aloud in Zulu as she pushed her on the swing: *kunye, kubile, kathathu, kune …*

Rachel and Siri on swing, Jeannette far right, Durban, 1950

To begin with, there were five bedrooms, but another bedroom was eventually created by converting one end of the upstairs veranda into a room for Jeannette. She and Kirstin were very different in their tastes and habits. According to Kirstin, Jeannette was too messy for her to tolerate. In one house we lived in, she drew an imaginary line down the middle of the room. Jeannette and her clothes and books were to stay on her own side of the line. Kirstin was somewhat formidable, even though she was only five feet tall, "and an eighth of an inch," as she would emphasize. She was very smart and graduated first in her class, earning the prestigious title, "Dux" of the school, at Durban Girls College.

Kirstin and Jeannette at new house, Durban, South Africa, 1949

Jeannette was taller than Kirstin. She had such a lovely figure. I remember the time we took our measurements: 36-24-36 was considered perfect. While she and I had exactly the same measurements, close to, but not completely, perfection, her height made all the difference to the result. When she walked past the boys playing cricket at Berea Park on the way to visit friends, she invariably attracted wolf whistles. Both girls had red hair, Kirstin's a dark auburn, very curly. Jeannette's straight hair was lighter, more strawberry blonde. My hair was often described as "ginger."

Siri and I happily shared a room until our older sisters left home. We were glad for the company. We didn't have many possessions, just dolls and a few small plastic cars, until the year we were given a doll house for Christmas. Everyone in the family worked on it, keeping it a secret until it was ready. We loved that little house. It had a real working front doorbell that hooked up to a battery. Dad later used the same pattern to make doll houses for his granddaughters.

Mike treasured his prism, his compass, his penknife, and his top. He liked marbles, too. His bedroom was next to ours and opened up onto the verandah, like ours did. The time he fell out of a tree and broke both his arms we could hear him moaning all through the night. Mike had white blonde hair and blue eyes, lots of freckles, too. He was absent-minded, always thinking, and once he even walked into a tree. He has always been interested in science and astronomy: he says he and Dad used to argue with Kirstin about different aspects of evolution.

Jeannette and Michael on Pehr's 3rd floor balcony, Durban, South Africa, 1949

Pehr was given the room at the top of the house on the third floor. He enjoyed the solitude, away from the rest of the family. In addition to photography, he had a stamp collection, encouraged and sponsored by our grandfather. He installed an old telescope on the railing of one of the little balconies that jutted out from his room and taught us everything he knew about the stars and how to identify the constellations, the Southern Cross, the Little Dipper, and Orion and his belt. We liked looking at the ships in the harbor and, my favorite, the moon. When we returned to America, I confidently informed my science teacher that the moon was upside down in the U.S. She didn't believe me. Years later I read an article in my children's *Odyssey* magazine explaining why the moon looked different in the Southern Hemisphere. I mailed a copy to that teacher, and she phoned to thank me for enlightening her. I find an interesting gap in people's understanding of the difference between the Northern and Southern hemispheres. I frequently have to remind even well-educated friends that the seasons are opposite, with summer in December in the Southern Hemisphere.

Pehr bought a shortwave radio so he could listen to the BBC news. He wanted to be sure he learned what was really going on in South African politics since news was censored and there was no television in South Africa at that time. He climbed up onto the roof and attached a radio aerial to one of the chimneys, alongside the lightning rod. He was subsequently informed that he shouldn't have been climbing about on brick tiles as they can easily crack. The radio beeped and squeaked loudly until he got the dial in the right position. I will never forget the first time I heard the sound of Big Ben tolling the hour all the way from London, eight thousand miles away. It sent shivers up my back.

The stairs up to Pehr's aerie were steep and curved. Being a resourceful sort of person who tinkered with tools and understood electricity, Pehr hooked up an electrical buzzer under some of the steps going up to his room to give fair warning of any little intruders planning to invade his territory. That worked well until Mike grew big enough to stretch his legs up over the bugged steps. I remember trying to jump over them myself, without success. In the linen closet under the stairs up to the third floor there was a box of homeopathic medicines Mother had brought from America. The tiny sugar pills tasted like candy. Mother was not happy when she discovered we had been raiding her precious supply. She had grown up in a town where homeopathy was practiced, and she firmly believed in the value of some of those medicines, especially arnica for bruises, aches, and pains, and chamomilla for teething.

Indian Mynah birds nested in the gutters outside Pehr's room. These birds have a yellow ring around their eyes. They are the kind of birds that pirates taught to say "pieces of eight." They scrabbled and fought, creating such a din that it disturbed him when he was studying. One day he took his pellet gun and shot at them, hoping to scare them into finding another place to nest. Instead, whenever Pehr walked outside, those intelligent birds dive-bombed him—never anyone else, just Pehr—they knew who had been shooting at them. While we were sometimes jealous of Pehr's private turret-like room, it was cold up there in the winter. He used to come down to dinner and put his cold hands around my neck, causing me to shriek.

There was a small door that opened off of Pehr's bedroom into an attic space directly above Kirstin's room. One time, when a group of young people from America was staying with us, Pehr and another boy, Feodor, took all the alarm clocks in the house and set them to ring at different times during the night. They placed the clocks on the floor of the attic. As Kirstin was notoriously grouchy when she was awakened, both she and her guest roommates were furious. Nowadays the story about the alarm clocks brings lots of laughter because, in the end, Kirstin married Feodor.

One reason the church bought such a big home for us was because there was a large room connected to the house that could be used as a church. Originally a music room, it had lots of windows and French doors that opened up to the outside. The plastered ceiling was decorated with an ornate pattern. With the addition of a wooden altar and communion rails, and red velvet curtains in the bay window, the big, airy room served us well as a church. The black and white-tiled hallway between the church and the rest of the house was a great place to roller skate. The noise reverberated against the walls and drove our Mother to tears. Jeannette, who was somewhat of a tomboy, broke her coccyx when she fell while roller skating.

I spent many hours practicing the piano in that church, and maybe one or two hours attempting to play the violin. It was my grandfather's violin and hadn't been played in decades. The instrument needed to be restrung, and the horsehair on the bow needed replacing. We were all relieved when my parents concluded that they couldn't afford to repair the instrument and pay for my lessons too. I did better with the piano: I competed in Welsh Eisteddfod music competitions, and my piano teacher required that I sit for the Royal College of Music examinations in music theory. These two institutions sent examiners out from the UK. I also played the hymns for church services.

Miriam, our Zulu cook, picked juicy, ripe papaya for Dad's breakfast every morning from the trees that planted themselves in a row along the wall outside the kitchen door where Mother threw the seeds out. We also had a couple of avocado trees, or "avocado pear" trees, as they were called. When the fruits became heavy, they sometimes dropped onto the ground and split open.

Rachel playing the piano in the Church, Durban, 1958

There was a laundry and a tool room down the hall from the kitchen, and a small powder room near the back door. We were supposed to wash our hands at the sink inside the back door after coming inside. Pehr had been instructed to smell our hands to make sure we used soap—after all, there were parasites in the soil, like the ones that caused amoebic dysentery, and there was hookworm, or "sand worm," a big problem for children who went about barefoot as we all did. I was particularly susceptible to sand worm. The painful, red, itchy welts grew longer and longer up my leg as the thing crawled under my skin from the bottom of my foot. It was difficult to treat, so Mother tried all sorts of remedies. She got some ideas from South African ladies, many of whom were superstitious but also passed along a number of useful folk remedies. Once she even tried painting my leg with shellac, the idea being that it would suffocate the larva. Children who sit in sandboxes that are contaminated by cat or dog feces are liable to get sandworm on their feet or buttocks. We didn't have a sandbox, but the soil under our shady mango trees was very soft, and no grass grew there.

The laundry, next to the kitchen, was light and airy and smelled of soap and a hot iron. Mother had employed various African laundresses over the years, but she ironed Dad's linen minister's robes herself. Sometimes Nellie, one of Siri's nannies, did the ironing.

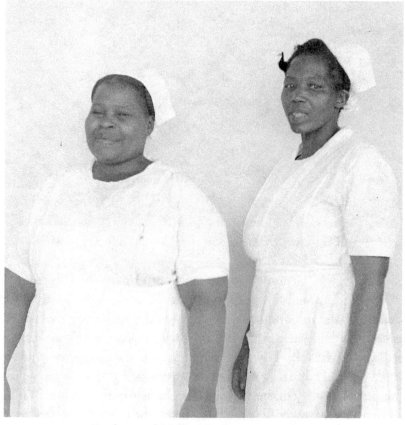

Sophie and Nellie, Siri's nannies, 1950

Mother had brought her front-loading Bendix washing machine from America. On a shelf above the laundry tub there were little blue cakes of Reckitt's Bluing that she added to the wash water to whiten clothes before putting them out in the sun to bleach. Tropical sun is so strong that hospitals put clean, scrubbed beds on the roof to kill any lingering germs.

There was a big, old-fashioned coal-burning stove in one corner of the laundry, which explains the extra chimney in the picture of the house. We once kept some chicks in the laundry. The baby chicks peeped loudly and grew quickly. I don't know what happened to them. We children thought they would be installed in the old chicken coop at the back of the garden, but they mysteriously disappeared. Perhaps Dad was afraid one of them would be a rooster? He was intolerant of any kind of noise, especially roosters crowing and cats yowling at night. There was a problem with a rooster kept by the servants at the apartment house in front of us. After a confrontation, followed by a meeting with the manager, the rooster disappeared. As for the cats, they liked the narrow passage that ran along behind the apartments' garages. Dad tried to scare them away by throwing rocks at them (he kept a little tin full of them on his bedroom windowsill). However, this did no good as we had a tall fence at the front of the house covered with thick bougainvillea vines that were planted to give our house some privacy. The stones didn't go through the thick vines.

Another example of a noise nuisance involved the "woo-wit" woman. An African woman, she sat on the sidewalk outside our house with her back against the warm red brick wall, calling out, "woo-wit," over and over again, all day long. Mom and Dad were reluctant to call the authorities when they found out that she was pregnant. Dad was ever aware of situations that might reflect badly on the church, so he didn't want to just leave her there. Instead, they brought her to stay in the servants' quarters, where she lived until she gave birth. Weeks later, she was back, with her baby, sitting against the brick wall, calling out "woo-wit" again. Siri and I once watched her feed the baby *phutu,* a kind of porridge. She took little bits of the soaked maize with her fingers, mashed them together, and put it in the baby's mouth. It looked uninviting, but was probably nutritious for the child. This time, for her sake and for the welfare of her child, a social service agency was called to take her away.

Next to the laundry was the tool room. A big wooden tool bench took up one side of the room. Pehr used it as a darkroom when he developed his film. He screwed a red light bulb into a hanging socket and turned it on when he was working so he would not destroy the negatives with bright light. It was also the room where Mike got up to some of his mischief. He told us how he made a sulfur "bomb" by putting a little pile of yellow sulfur powder in a metal lid and then placing it under an open window where Dad was conducting an evening doctrinal class (Bible study) in his study. When he lit the powder, it produced a terrible odor. He and his friends also made gunpowder. Another act of treason he conducted was with Pehr: they lit firecrackers outside the windows just as a little old lady plugged in the electric kettle to make tea for the study group.

In addition to the washing machine, Mother shipped her Frigidaire refrigerator and her Mixmaster to South Africa. These appliances had to be plugged into transformers since the voltage was higher than in the U.S. Most people didn't have electric mixers. When I made cookies or cakes with my friends, we mixed the butter and sugar with our hands. The freezer in the fridge was just big enough for two ice trays. Since the milk that was delivered to the house every morning was not homogenized, Mother made ice cream from the cream that rose to the top of the milk. She collected the cream until she had enough to make Sunday dessert for the family. Mixed with sugar, and sometimes crushed fruit, the ice cream was poured into the empty metal ice tray, where it had to be stirred several times to prevent ice crystals from forming. She served it with her own thick, fudgy, chocolate sauce that sometimes turned hard on the ice cream.

The ice cream sold in Durban was nothing like American ice cream. There was a choice of chocolate, vanilla, or "pink" ice cream, supposedly strawberry or cherry flavored. South African ice cream was much derided by the older children in the family who remembered Breyers ice cream and delectable American treats like ice cream sodas.

There were several garages on the grounds. The larger one, a double garage, was converted into a study for Dad. The servants lived behind these garages. Our cook, Miriam Nyandu, lived in a room on one side, and our male servant, Piet Mkhize, the gardener or "boy," as he would have been called, on the other side. There was also a garage for the car and, at the very back, a separate garage where discarded furniture and other junk was kept. The servants' rooms, called *kaias*, were dark and smelled musty and damp. They all used the same shower and toilet. For some reason, there was no door to their bathroom. The toilet, a hole in the ground, was lined with ceramic but the floor was concrete and I worried about how easily someone could slip into that hole. It was clean and smelled of Dettol disinfectant. We were taught not to invade our servants' privacy so we rarely ventured back there.

Garage before converted to study, Durban, 1949

We had two bathrooms in the house at 185, one was the "girls' bathroom" and the other, off our parents' bedroom, was designated as the "boys' bathroom." The girls' bathroom had a toilet with a pull chain flushing mechanism. This noisy contraption was very different from what we were accustomed to. The chain was pulled several times and then water from a tank attached to the wall would flow down a pipe and empty the toilet bowl. The boys' bathroom was new, so they had a regular lever flush mechanism. These kinds of things were of great interest to Mike. Dad used to shower all three of us together, Michael, Siri, and me, after we went swimming at the beach. One day he told me I had to use the girls' bathroom from then on. I was quite put out and didn't understand that Mike was growing up, embarrassed to be seen by his sister. The boys' bathroom smelled of Lifebuoy soap and the Bay Rum Dad used as an aftershave. We used our mother's sweet-smelling Cashmere Bouquet soap.

Because you had to walk through our parents' bedroom to reach the bathroom, guests of either gender used the girls' room. One day, her dark brown eyes sparkling, Siri arrived at the dinner table and announced that she'd had a bath, "full to the top." She had climbed into our American guest's bath after he was finished. Perhaps it had a slow drain. We were allowed only a couple of inches of water because the hot water heater wouldn't serve so many people otherwise. The guest was very embarrassed. It was Mother's turn to shrink when Siri went on to tell this same guest (it was Feodor, again) that Mother had put all the shabby and broken furniture in the storage garage just before he came. Siri also complained to him that she had only one pair of pajamas, which was quite true.

Tennis court prior to renovation, Durban, South Africa, 1949

To add to the one-time grandeur of 185, there was a clay tennis court in the back yard. When we moved in, it was in very run-down condition—there was a tree growing up in the middle of it. There was also a WWII air raid shelter, next to the tennis court. I don't think there were many other houses with bomb shelters in the city of Durban even though there had been a real danger from German U-boats patrolling off the coast. (The Germans hoped to prevent the Japanese from forming a naval base on Madagascar.) We dared each other to go down into that dark, damp, space and then tried to imagine what it would be like to sleep in there with the spiders. The hard, cold, concrete bench wouldn't have made a comfortable bed. The shelter was eventually filled in for fear it would collapse.

SUNDAY DINNERS

Family at dinner table (note brass tray on mantelpiece in background), Durban, South Africa, 1951

The family always sat down together for Sunday dinner after church. Mother was experienced at planning the meal so everything would be ready to serve at the right time, even though she attended the church service. She laid out a white tablecloth and her gilt-edged Limoges china with the little forget-me-not flowers, together with the family silver. We all sat down at the big cherry dining table that had once graced her grandmother's stately home in Toronto. Sometimes she used a crocheted lace tablecloth that hurt when you put your elbows on it. Once, when Michael was told to take his elbows off the table, he replied that Mr. Royston, our guest, had *his* elbows on the table, so why shouldn't he? Mr. R. sheepishly removed his elbows.

Other than the Royal Hotel there weren't many restaurants in Durban where you could entertain guests, so our Sunday dinners frequently included a member of the congregation or a guest from out of town. Whole families occasionally stayed with us, travelling down from Zimbabwe or Johannesburg. But my favorite guest was Meg.

MARGARET MARY

Margaret Mary, or Meg, came to live with us at Sydenham Road when I was about fourteen. She had met Pehr at the University of Natal, and he introduced her to the family. When she became ill, her mother was worried about her making the long commute from their farm on Natal's north coast, so Mother invited her to stay with us. I was thrilled—Meg was adventurous and fun, with a great imagination. She was studying art at the time she lived with us. The two of us took long walks early in the morning and took it in turns to describe the imaginary families living in the quiet, sleeping houses we passed. When she turned twenty-one, her parents gave her a little blue Austin so she could drive herself around and visit them at the farm on weekends. (Driver's licenses were issued at age twenty-one.)

Meg had attended a finishing school in Switzerland, something that was expected of a very proper British farmer's daughter. It was when she was in Switzerland that she first heard about Swedenborg and the New Church. When she mentioned this at college, a friend told her, "Oh, you must meet with Pehr Odhner. He knows about Swedenborg, too." Even though she had learned how she should behave, Meg was occasionally quite rebellious. Her mother was upset to hear that her daughter was interested in a religion other than the Church of England. She came to tea at our house to check on what the church taught, fearing we might be some kind of a cult.

Margaret Mary (Meg) Siri, and Jeannette by Meg's little blue Austin, Durban, South Africa, 1957

Meg was tall and elegant. She was seven years older than I am, about the same age as my sister, Jeannette. She always sat with her long legs slanted to one side, never crossed, which was unladylike, she said. I tried to imitate her, but my legs were just too short. She introduced me to Vivaldi and Vaughan Williams, Clementi, and Respighi, all so different from the music Dad liked. When Meg and I sat in the cool, dark church in the evenings and listened to music on the church's record player, she would tell me to close my eyes while listening to the music so I could really appreciate it.

She would "oh" and "ah" and take my hand and say, "That was so beautiful! Did you hear that?" in her very proper English accent. She sounds just like Joanna Lumley, who so beautifully narrates the TV series, *Greek Odyssey*. Dad preferred Brahms and Beethoven, and the *New World* symphony by Dvorak. Someone gave us a recording of Rossini's *William Tell* Overture which he especially enjoyed playing as it reminded him of the *Lone Ranger* radio broadcasts he had listened to in America. Mother preferred Strauss waltzes. Sometimes we moved the record player out of the church and listened to music in our living room. We also had a Grundig radio. I used to sit close to it, my ear next to the speaker, and listen to the popular music of the day, which was not acceptable to my parents. I needed to be "in the know" about the Top Ten "hits." My parents were horrified at Elvis Presley. My friends at school said things like, "All Americans sleep with a picture of Elvis under their pillows." I wish to emphasize that there was no television, no internet, and there were no cell phones. They got their ideas from magazines, I suppose.

Music room used for church, 185 Sydenham Road, Mike standing in front, Durban, South Africa, 1956

Meg had friends who were political activists in the underground political movements. She once took me to a party where a group of liberal young men and women were engaged in lively discussions about the situation in their country. One of them, his name was Ian, was "banned" because of his anti-apartheid activities. That meant that he couldn't leave his home or participate in any meetings, must resign his job and, virtually, become a non-person. Meg was much saddened by this. I remember that she took him food on some occasions.

Careful with her appearance, she was one of the first people I knew who wore contact lenses. Meg had "mousy brown hair" that had been blonde when she was young. She tied it up in a soft bun on the back of her head. The two of us once decided to wash our hair with Sunlight soap, which was actually a harsh laundry soap but we'd heard it would put highlights in your hair. It was a disaster. The hair stuck out all over, like dry grass, so we looked like scarecrows, or perhaps like a sucked mango pip (Meg's own description). We washed and re-washed our hair with real shampoo afterwards to try to get it back to a normal texture.

I recently found some old letters from Meg in which she described how much she loved listening to music with me. She reminded me of the cascading branches of yellow flowers on the cassia tree Mother had planted outside the church windows. She wrote of the smell of summer, "warm and sultry, lovely."

"In the short time that I knew everybody at 185 Sydenham Road, there was so much joy, so much learning for me," she wrote.

THE PARSONAGE PARTY

One year my parents agreed to make our house available for my class party. We were centrally located, the front terrace was perfect for dancing, and the pillars lent an elegance not to be found at any of my friends' houses. Attracted by the music and the strings of colored lights, several inebriated young men, "teddy boys," came over from the nearby Ocean View Hotel and crashed the party. They persuaded some of the girls to walk off into the back yard with them. There were a couple of girls in my class who were more sophisticated than the rest of us when it came to dating and boys, so perhaps it had been pre-arranged. Dad went around rooting the couples out of the bushes and demanding, loudly, that the young men should leave.

Somehow, this story attracted the attention of a newspaper reporter, who headlined it as the "Parsonage Party" on the first page of the next morning's edition of the *Natal Mercury*. The name of our school, Durban Girls College, was mentioned, too, so my very embarrassed father found himself apologizing to the headmistress, Miss Middleton.

The grand old house on Sydenham Road served many purposes: family home; church and offices; theological school, and social center for family, friends, and church members. But now, looking at the photographs, comparing its size to the rough rural dwellings of the African ministers, I feel a sad discomfort. A few years after we returned to America, the house was torn down. Access to the property was blocked when they sunk Sydenham Road to ease traffic at the intersection with Musgrave Road. The road has a new name, John Zikhali Road. But they left some of the mango trees.

Driving past that empty space distorts the memory, as if we could never have lived there. But if you stand quietly, you can just hear the echo of children's voices lingering under the mango trees like a low-lying fog that moves along the ground, ghostlike.

———⟫●⟪———

THE POPULATION REGISTRATION ACT, ACT NO 30 OF 1950

To make provision for the compilation of a Register of the Population of the Union; for the issue of Identity Cards to persons whose names are included in the Register.

Until this Act of 1950, people could "pass" from one group to a more privileged one if their physical features made this possible.

The Act required people to be identified and registered from birth as one of four distinct racial groups: White; Coloured; Bantu (Black African), and other. It was one of the "pillars" of apartheid. Race was reflected in the individual's Identity Number. An Office for Race Classification was established. The wording was imprecise, but it was applied with great enthusiasm:

A White person is one who is in appearance obviously white—and not generally accepted as Coloured—or who is generally accepted as White—and is not obviously Non-White, provided that a person shall not be classified as a White person if one of his natural parents has been classified as a Coloured person or a Bantu...

A Bantu is a person who is, or is generally accepted as, a member of any aboriginal race or tribe of Africa... [Later amended to replace the designation "Bantu" with "Black."]

A Coloured is a person who is not a White person or a Bantu...

A fourth category—**Asian (Indian and Pakistani)**—was later added.

THE COLOR TRIBUNAL

He will appear by appointment at a bleak room near the centre of Cape Town. Two or three members of the tribunal will sit, in the accepted fashion, with their backs to the rather inadequate light... Descriptions are taken of the colour and texture of hair, eyes, skin and bone structure of the face, and searching inquiries are made about ancestry, associations, social habits. The fact that no satisfactory definition of race has ever been formulated is, of course, ignored. A feat that would baffle any known anthropologist is expected of comparatively minor civil servants. [Owen Williams, *Africa South*][4]

What are the effects of the pass laws on the lives of Africans?

The possibility of summary arrest for non-production of his reference book on demand haunts the African night and day. His every move is subject to unceasing control. His choice of work and of employer are restricted. He has little or no hope of advancement, nor can he change his type of work. He cannot obtain a house or pension, etc., unless he has a reference book. His family life is constantly disrupted, causing, among other things, an increase in illegitimacy and crime.

Money for food becomes money for fines, and whether the offender pays the fine, reducing his poor earnings to even less, or goes to jail, thereby rendering himself unable to support his family, the results are the same—poverty, malnutrition, disease, and the complete breakdown of family life. [*The Black Sash*][5]

Memorandum on the Pass Laws

The pass laws are being evermore rigidly applied and more and more people are being affected by their implementation. .... In the year July 1970 to June 1971, **615,075 people** were prosecuted for pass law offences; that is, an average of 1,685 prosecutions per day. [The Black Sash, *Reality*] [6]

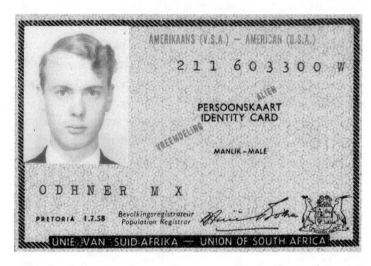

Michael's identity card, issued two months after his 16th birthday

CHAPTER 2

EUROPEANS ONLY

The house at 185 Sydenham Road, or "185," as we have referred to it for many years, was located only a few blocks from our schools. Pehr attended Durban High School, and Michael went to Durban Preparatory School, both "government" schools (what are called public schools in America). Kirstin started at Girls High School. Jeannette was unhappy at her new primary school on Berea Road—the teacher hit her hand with a ruler when she didn't know an Afrikaans word, even though she hadn't learned the language yet. When I was five years old, I attended a little church school, Kainon School. In the end, all four of us girls attended Durban Girls College, an excellent British private school of about five hundred girls from Kindergarten through Sixth Form (Twelfth Grade).

We lived close enough to walk to the school, but I didn't like walking to school because of the vicious dogs people kept in their yards to scare away black people and burglars. I would cross the road several times in order to avoid them, even though they were safely behind strong gates. When we didn't walk to school, we rode the municipal bus, the big red double-decker bus you see on London streets in the movies. One of the stories my sister Jeannette told us is about her first encounter with the bench at the bus stop.

It was shortly after we had moved to the Sydenham Road house, so she was about ten years old when she walked down to the bus stop, carrying her school suitcase. She would have passed the nasturtiums mother planted along the driveway, each of their round umbrella-shaped leaves capturing one perfect jewel of dew in the middle. Jeannette was tall for her age, freckle-faced, her hair a lovely shade of light auburn. She tugged on the uncomfortable elastic under her chin that held her white panama hat in place. The wide brim shaded her face from the sun. Part of her school uniform, the green and white grosgrain ribbon around the crown of the hat matched her "bottle green" dress. Uniforms had to be worn the right way. Jeannette was caught without her hat by the headmistress one afternoon when walking home from school. She was told to put the hat back on, as it was part of her uniform. Miss Middleton drove off. Jeannette again removed her hat. Miss Middleton returned—she had driven around the block, knowing Jeannette would do just that. Unlike me, Jeannette wasn't afraid of the strictness at our school. She thought it was fun to spend an hour in detention after school with her friends.

Heading for the bus stop that first day, she carefully skirted the sticky spot on the sidewalk where flying ants gathered under the streetlight overnight and, now wingless, had fallen to the pavement to be squashed by passing feet. She could hear the nimble little Indian boys as they darted around and between cars that had stopped at the intersection of Sydenham and Musgrave Roads. They were calling out the price of the morning paper, the *Natal Mercury*: "Sixpence, please, sixpence!" hoping to catch the drivers before they started up again.

When she reached the bus stop, she noticed the black and white metal sign screwed into one of the slats on the back of the wooden bench: *Europeans Only*. There were a few "native girls" (as they were referred to), nannies, perhaps, standing behind the bench in the shade of a colorful bougainvillea vine that draped over the brick wall behind them. The day gets hot very quickly on summer mornings in Durban. Sunrise is at five a.m. Since the city is near the Tropic of Capricorn, there are equal days and nights so it gets dark quickly in the evening. There is no lingering summer evening twilight with fireflies.

Not knowing what a European was, Jeannette didn't know what to do, she says, so she stood next to the African women, behind the bench. Another girl, already sitting on the bench, asked her why she didn't sit down. Jeannette replied, "Because I'm not a European."

The sign was also printed in Afrikaans: *Slegs Blankes*. She didn't know that meant Whites Only. She had seen the same words in other places. Who, or what was a "European"? She stood there, uncomfortable, looking down at her feet, waiting for the bus, which ground its gears loudly as it came up the slope toward the Sydenham Road bus stop.

At our British school the social studies curriculum was focused on England and the British Empire. We learned about places and products, "boots and shoes," as Mother called it. We read about coal and Newcastle upon Tyne; Stonehenge; and all the kings named Henry, Richard, and George. In geography class we heard about the romantic-sounding Canterbury Plains in the faraway British Commonwealth colony of New Zealand.

We learned firsthand about the Suez Canal when it was closed in 1956 and fleets of international shipping anchored off the coast, waiting for a berth in Durban Harbor. In church, we learned about heaven and hell, and Joseph, with his coat of many colors. We were warned that children in heaven get spots on their clothes and their flowers droop if they do not tell the truth.

As we grew older, we studied wars and treaties, and English literature—Shakespeare, Jane Austen, and Sir Walter Scott. When we discussed the Crusades, we were not taught that the Crusades were essentially wrong-headed for, after all, Richard the Lionheart was an English king. In South African history class, we read about the Zulu wars which, they emphasized, proved that the Zulus were only just then moving southwards when the English were moving north, and because the English won the battles, therefore the land was theirs. In church we learned about Divine providence, and what the little figures in the Christmas representation mean—there shouldn't be a donkey or a cow in the scene, only a horse, said Dad, because a horse signifies understanding.

Even though we learned some abstract ideas, there was one subject that was never talked about, as far as I can remember, not at school, not in church, nor within the family: racism. It was a situation taken for granted. "Whites were conditioned to regard apartheid society as normal, its critics as communists or communist sympathizers.[7]" In those days, race in South Africa could be determined simply by whether a pencil fell out of your curly hair or not. Truly. Using that measuring stick, close family members could be officially declared as belonging to different races. While everyone could ride the bus, when it came to sitting on a bench, the white race trumped all others, in two words, in black and white: *Europeans Only.*

I recently suggested to my son, who lives in Auckland, New Zealand (a British Commonwealth country, as South Africa was when we lived there), that he should ask his ten-year old daughter if she knows what a European is. The school she attends has a widely diverse student body. She replied, not at all sure, "An English person?" I suggested that he put a sign on a chair, "Europeans Only," and ask her if she would sit there. He said she became confused—just as her great-aunt Jeannette had, more than sixty years earlier.

RESERVATION OF SEPARATE AMENITIES ACT, ACT NO 49 OF 1953

The Act forced segregation in all public amenities, public buildings, and public transport with the aim of eliminating contact between whites and other races. "Europeans Only" and "Non-Europeans Only" signs were put up... facilities provided for different races need not be equal.

Educational apartheid was enforced in schools, colleges, and universities. African schooling was neither free nor compulsory, as it was for whites.

**SELFLESS, COMMITTED DOCTOR KEPT
THE FAITH FOR FREEDOM AND EQUITY
JAY SADHAI, DOCTOR,
ANTI-APARTHEID CAMPAIGNER**

The late Dr. Jay Sadhai emigrated to Australia from South Africa in 1977. He tells this story in his autobiography, *Bala's Hill and Beyond*. For Jay, it is "the most striking single and extreme experience of apartheid's cruel madness." [Dr. Sadhai was an Indian.]

Called by telephone to attend a reported sea drowning, he was confronted on arrival at the beach by a large 'Whites Only' sign, and was collared by a policeman, who prevented him from giving assistance to a young white boy in distress. Jay had to stand and watch from a distance as the boy died—the whites-only ambulance the policeman had called arrived too late to help. [J. Nieuwenhuysen, *The Age*, Australia][8]

"This is a White republic, ruled by the white man, part of the white domain of the world, but with full understanding for the ambitions and objectives of the Black man of Africa within our own midst."[9] [Hendrik F. Verwoerd, 1966]

CHAPTER 3

FEAR OF WHAT THE DARK CONCEALS

Like a lot of young children, Siri and I were afraid to go upstairs by ourselves in the dark, so most nights our older brother Pehr went with us. He was usually on his way upstairs, anyway, to study for his college classes. He was big and strong and, to my mind, he wasn't afraid of anything. I always admired his hands: he could snap his middle finger onto his thumb and make a very loud noise. The house at 185 Sydenham Road had very high ceilings, an advantage in hot weather, but it meant lots of steps going up to the second floor, twenty-five steps in all. Stamping our feet loudly on the uncarpeted stairs gave us courage, and would surely scare away the burglars. Pehr went up first, leaping two or three steps at a time, leaving us behind. For a moment, his shadow moved along the wall in the dim upstairs hall. I would freeze, but only for a moment, because that happened every time. It was mostly Pehr's fault that we were afraid—he loved to tell stories at the dinner table, about burglars, or the Mau Mau terrorists in Kenya. He seemed to enjoy it, much to Mother's distress. I had no idea at the time that Kenya was more than two thousand miles away from where we lived.

Our bedroom, Siri's and mine, was at the top of the stairs. A second door and a window opening onto the veranda were left open to catch the sea breeze in the evening. The veranda partly encircled the second floor. Americans would call it a sleeping porch. That house had lots of doors, both upstairs and down. There were eight doors downstairs that Dad made sure to lock every night. He locked the downstairs windows, too, and pulled out all the electrical plugs. He had served as a volunteer fireman for years, and the high voltage South African electricity worried him. He'd had too much experience with house fires.

We didn't have wrought iron burglar guards on our windows like most of our neighbors did. After one burglary, where it was obvious how the thief got into our house—the police found dirty shoeprints on the wall beneath the window—they added burglar guards to that window. I was sleeping in that room when the burglar entered. One night, as she went to bed, as the result of some kind of premonition, Mother took all the cash out of her purse, which she kept in a drawer in the front hall chest. Wrapping the money in a scarf, she stuffed it into the back of the drawer. That night, a thief got into the house, took her purse outside onto the terrace, and dumped the contents out in the moonlight. He must have been frustrated when he found there was no money.

For security, they installed a strange contraption at the end of the ledge by the upstairs verandah. It was shaped like an isosceles triangle with barbed wire wrapped around it. Hopefully, it would discourage anyone from getting around that corner. The flat roof the burglars used to gain access to our living quarters also gave my brother Mike a way of looking in the window when an elderly, and very plump, parishioner was using the upstairs bathroom after church one day. It must have been assumed that a burglar would have a hard time getting in through the small bathroom windows, but I think a child could have done it, with a boost up.

When we reached the upstairs hallway, Pehr switched on the dim overhead light in our bedroom. I urged Siri to jump onto her bed from as far away as she could—it had to be a running jump for it to be far enough—because what if someone was waiting under the bed and could reach out and grab our ankles? The bedsprings creaked and jangled as we giggled, nervously, safely out of the way of whatever I could imagine might be there. As we went barefoot most of the time, Siri remembers the feeling of her sticky feet under the clean, white cotton sheets that smelled so nice and fresh because Mother hung them outdoors to dry. After turning out our light, Pehr climbed the narrow, winding staircase to his own room on the third floor. It took many, many years for some of us to overcome the fear of thieves in the night.

Pehr studied at a big, square oak desk that had been shipped from America. Mother called it "the Uncle Louis desk." Uncle Louis Pendleton, Mother's great-uncle, wrote about the history of the Southern states. He was best known for his biography of Alexander Stephens, Vice President of the Confederacy during the American Civil War. Stephens was from Georgia, as was our Pendleton family. Mother's grandfather, William Frederic Pendleton, had served as a Captain in the Confederate army (he later became a Swedenborgian bishop) which horrified us and became a contentious talking point whenever we discussed the Battle of Gettysburg. Dad's grandfather, Charles Xandry, had served as a Union soldier at Gettysburg. Our Pendleton great aunts told of how the Union Army under General Sherman bayoneted their down quilts and poured honey all over them, leaving the family to label the mess as "Sherman pies."

Once when I went up to Pehr's room to call him to dinner, I looked over his shoulder and asked him about the book he was reading. It was *Beowulf*. I was fascinated by the look and sound of the strange Old English words as he read some of it aloud to me. He was eleven years older than me, and I thought everything he did was amazing. Years later, I studied Beowulf in college myself.

As I lay in the dark I couldn't help thinking about what Pehr had told us at the dinner table that night about the Mau Mau terrorists who were rebelling against white colonial rule in Kenya. The Mau Mau wanted all whites to leave, even if they had to destroy the farms and murder all the farmers. At least that was the story spread around by the British rulers of Kenya colony at the time. Pehr recounted how the terrorists put slivers of wood up your fingernails if they caught you. Mother had shushed him with a stern, "Pehr!" shaking her head sharply from side to side, her mouth a thin line of disapproval. But now we were upstairs, alone, in the dark. I curled up my fists with the fingernails tightly closed in against the palm of my hand—then they wouldn't be able to stick the splinters in while I slept.

On the hottest summer nights, I liked to sleep on the verandah. You could look at the stars twinkling, mirrored by the city lights below. Ships in the harbor were lighted, too. On New Year's Eve, at midnight, all the ships sounded their foghorns. It was very dramatic. The only disadvantage to sleeping on the verandah was that the sun woke you up at five in the morning. Dad complained that it shone on his big toe, the toe that suffered from painful bouts of gout, waking him. We didn't have window blinds or shades, just some rather skimpy curtains. Decorating the house was not first on the list of priorities with a big family living on a minister's income. Meg, the art student I mentioned in the first chapter, designed some beautiful cloth that Mother sewed into curtains for the dining room. The background was a dark burgundy red, patterned with fanciful long-tailed birds, rather like pheasants.

One night, after everyone had gone to bed, there was a loud pounding on the front door. Then the doorbell rang, insistently. Dad picked up the long flashlight he always kept by his bed and went down the stairs into the front hall. The rest of us stayed at the top of the stairs. The opaque leaded glass in the door blurred the view of anyone standing outside. It was old and bowed out a little—it would be easy to punch it in. It didn't help that the outside light above the front door was dim, the domed glass shade full of the ubiquitous dead flying ants.

In answer to Dad's shouted query, "Who's there?" a man replied, "Mfundisi, me bloken man!" He said he was being chased and pleaded to be let into the house. Perhaps he had seen the Church's sign out front, the black wooden sign with the name of the church on it in gold letters. The man had called him by the Zulu word for minister, *Mfundisi*. He must have trusted that a minister would give him refuge. But Dad was worried about who might be chasing the man. Or was it a trick? Perhaps he was pretending to be injured, to gain entry to the house. Why was he out at that time of night? There was a nine-p.m. curfew for non-whites, and it was well past that time. If the man had been beaten by a *skebenga*, a ruffian, he might have followed him to our house and would break down the door to get at him, putting the family in danger. On the other hand, if the police were chasing the wounded man, Dad could be accused of harboring a runaway criminal. Sometimes black men were beaten by black policemen, who carry hard rubber *sjamboks* they use to beat their victims.

Kirstin and Jeannette at front door. Note leaded glass in front door

Deeply conflicted, Dad didn't open the door. He left the man outside, hoping his pursuers had already abandoned him and he would get away safely. Calling in the police might cause the wounded man more problems. And, after all, he had not threatened us in any way. But would he be able to survive in his condition? We went back to bed, unsettled.

The next morning, when Piet went to sweep the front verandah, he saw bloody handprints on the white-painted pillars outside the front door and brought it to Dad's attention. The two of them searched around the property until they found more bloodstains on the low wall that separated our yard from the kaias where the servants who work in the flats lived. He must have jumped down there to hide or run away.

There was no newspaper report of a body being found.

There wouldn't have been.

There was no eulogy for a black man.

⟹●⟸

THE GROUP AREAS ACT,
ACT NO 41 OF 1950

Forced physical separation between races by creating different residential areas for different races. Led to forced removals of people living in "wrong" areas.

The purpose of the Group Areas Act is to provide for the establishment of separate areas for the different races in South Africa. Theoretically, it empowers the authorities to deal with all the races on the same basis. In practice, it exists for the purpose of removing the non-White people from their places of occupation in cities, towns, villages and farms. All plans for segregation, particularly those affecting the Indian people, show the desire on the part of the upholders of apartheid to rob them of their properties and other economic interests. In all cases the plans involve uprooting of settled populations and the deprivation of their means of livelihood. [Yusuf Cachalia, *Africa South*][10]

**DURBAN EXPLODES: RIOTS,
DEMONSTRATIONS, VIOLENCE**
DURBAN
Under the **Group Areas Act**, Cato [Manor] Africans, like so many non-whites throughout the Union, are being forcibly moved to wherever the authorities think fit.

As one African told me, "This is not slum clearance. It is human clearance." ... While many people were at work, they broke down shanties. Families came home from their white employers to find the only home and shelter they had lying in mess and rubble on the ground. Most of them had absolutely nowhere else to go...

The police, called in by Council officials, gave the women five minutes to disperse. The minutes were counted dramatically over a loudspeaker. Then suddenly the rushing of feet, the thin high screams of women, the hard fall of bodies. The police baton charge had begun. Shoes, some very down-and-out at the heel, made bumpy trails in the dust as the women threw them off in order to run more quickly from the clubbing batons. About 3,000 women were fleeing from the police fury; tear gas bombs exploded all around them. All at once, they heard the unmistakable rattle of stenguns firing. [Myrna Blumberg, *Africa South*][11]

**WIDOWS MUST LEAVE THEIR HOMES:
CITY COUNCIL REFUSES TO BUDGE**
JOHANNESBURG Widows who have refused to leave their houses have been subjected to interrogation by the municipal police who visit them day and night threatening that if they do not leave, they will be arrested. A paper carrier with only a few items of clothing was all that Mrs. Lekopatsa found in her house after she had served a jail sentence for refusing to carry out an order ejecting her from her house. Her house had been transferred to someone else, and all her furniture had been sold... . Mrs. Lekopotsa, of Naledi, who was imprisoned three times for failing to leave her home and served sentences ranging from one month to three, left the Republic last week for Basutoland with her three children. [*New Age*][12]

THE SOUTH AFRICAN WAY OF LIFE
"JUST PUT THEM IN A HOME"

A white woman from Durban married a St. Helena seaman in 1939. It was perfectly legal for her to do so then. But under present South African race classification laws he is regarded as Coloured. The woman had six children and she later divorced her husband. Three children have since married Coloured men. The woman has now remarried a white man. The children live with them—for the moment. Unfortunately, husband and wife are classified as white and the three children as Coloured. The Group Areas Act says white and Coloured may not live in the same area. What do the authorities suggest?

"Put the children in a home..."

[*Liberal Opinion*][13]

CHAPTER 4

GOVERNMENT SUGAR

I put my nose into the box of Domino's brown sugar and breathed in the delicious sweetness, unlike anything else I was acquainted with. The only kind of brown sugar available in South Africa was "government sugar," a pale beige sugar that was not fully processed. Cheaper than white sugar, it was intended only for "natives," so it was sold in plain, brown, unlabeled paper bags. Ironically, it is the same as today's trendy raw sugar served in some fancy restaurants in little brown paper packets.

We all looked forward to the packages our grandmother sent us from America. They provided an important connection to someone who loved us and to a country I didn't know. The boxes came by ship, taking up to three months to arrive. The "mail boat," a Union-Castle passenger liner, docked in Durban harbor on the same day each week, the crew blowing the foghorn to announce its arrival. The ships sailed from their home port, Southampton, in the United Kingdom. My father's parents had both passed away before he was ten years old, so our Caldwell grandparents are the only ones we've known personally, and because we younger ones grew up so far away from them, we didn't even know the Caldwells very well.

In addition to the brown sugar, Grandmother Caldwell sent the Sunday colored comics my older brothers and sisters remembered—*Nancy, Blondie,* and *Henry*. Mike remembers reading *Li'l Abner,* and *Dick Tracy.*

Dick Tracy had a character called "Fearless Fosdick," who always had lots of see-through bullet holes in his body, and Pehr thought this was terribly funny. I think Mother thought the comics were a bad influence and asked Granny to stop sending them. I remember that we all wrote letters to Granny one day. Mine had so many spelling errors that everyone thought it was so funny that, liking the attention, I offered to make copies with even more errors in them. [Michael Xandry Odhner]

Packed into the box with the brown sugar, there were tins of Bond Street tobacco for our pipe-smoking father and several magazines, something for each of us: The *Saturday Evening Post* for Dad, and *Ladies Home Journal* for Mother. Dad loved to read aloud C.S. Forester's *Hornblower* stories, serialized in the *Post*. Pehr looked forward to new issues of *Popular Mechanics,* and Mike, when he was younger, liked *Highlights for Children*. Jeannette and Kirstin enjoyed *Seventeen* magazine, and Siri and I shared *Jack and Jill.*

One year she sent us books—new books. It was my first new book, and it belonged to me. It was about Leif the Lucky, Leif Erikson, who sailed on his Viking ship from Greenland and landed on the coast of North America. We often teased our father, whose own father was Swedish, about being a Viking. I was fascinated by the aboriginal Newfoundlanders, called "skraelings" in the book. I could never have imagined such people, with their painted faces and feathers in their hair. It helped illustrate the story Mother told us about our ancestor, Rebecca Dean (my 5X great-grandmother) who was scalped and burned by Indians, along with her youngest children, in their cabin. They had settled in a remote place called Sinking Valley on the Juniata River in the Allegheny Mountains of central Pennsylvania. In 1780 that area was the western frontier of the American colony. According to a decree by William Penn, colonists weren't supposed to settle west of the Susquehanna River, but my ancestors moved there anyway. The British then stirred up the Indians to attack the settlers. Rebecca's daughter, from whom I am descended, married a Caldwell. She survived the raid because she was out working in the fields with her father and older siblings.

That book had a colorful illustrated paper cover and smelled clean, not like the library books we borrowed from the Durban Municipal Library that were dipped in formaldehyde to kill bookworms. Bookworms eat their way through a book from cover to cover, getting bigger along the way, and could devastate a collection if not caught in time. A tiny hole in the front of a book ended up as almost half an inch in diameter at the other end. Bookworms were a scourge: they laid eggs in the bindings. Experts have since discovered that freezing the book takes care of the worms. Books were also victims of cockroaches, which ate the glue in the covers, leaving a telltale fuzzy surface. And termites: they ate up the back of the big bookcase in Dad's study—he heard them one night when he was working late, a *click click* sound, and pulled the bookcase out from the wall. That resulted in the exterminators digging big holes all over our yard until they found the queen, a big jelly-like slug. People reported that after a house was treated for roaches, you could see the insects crossing the road in a long line, hoping to find a new home.

In addition to being treated for book worms, those Durban library books were all covered in black or dark green shiny cloth, to deter mildew. It was hard to be interested in a book that smelled like chemicals, especially when it looked just like every other book on the shelf. Plus, Mother had the habit of suggesting books she had enjoyed as a child, like *Beau Geste*, a 1924 adventure novel by P.C. Wren, which didn't appeal to me at all. She would become quite impatient with me. So I really appreciated Grandmother's gift.

Mother's study, which we called the library, held her big desk with its row of pigeon holes and two walls of bookcases filled with old books she had brought from America. I remember some of the titles: *1066 and All That*, a parody of English history published in 1930; *Plutarch's Lives;* and *You Are What You Eat*, a bright yellow paperback that would be at home on the shelves of our local health food store today. She says she read so much as a girl that when her mother limited her to one book a week, she sat up with a flashlight and read under the covers after going to bed.

Our grandparents sent money one year so Mother could buy a lemon tree. We were so excited when the tree finally flowered and produced fruit. We also planted a lychee tree. Lychees were a favorite fruit we associate with Christmas. Because of its seasonal nature, we found the fruit in our Christmas stockings, like the tangerine Mother used to have in her stocking as a child. The red prickly skin comes off cleanly, revealing juicy white flesh surrounding a big brown seed. Just the smell of a lychee, even a canned one, brings Christmas memories to mind. Lychee trees take seven years to bear fruit. Unfortunately, we moved away before we could enjoy ours.

Of all the things Grandmother sent, what I loved best were the Valentines. I had no idea what Saint Valentine's Day was, but I loved to run my fingers across the soft velvety surface of those flocked hearts. I look for flocked cards just like them to send my own grandchildren. In doing so I feel the deep pleasure she must have taken in choosing those cards especially for me. It's one way to thank her for creating such a special memory.

⟝⟞⟝●⟞⟝

THE DEFIANCE CAMPAIGN OF 1952

The "Campaign of Defiance Against Unjust Laws," was launched by the African National Congress of South Africa and the South African Indian Congress. A mass action passive resistance campaign, their goal was the abolition of the Pass Laws, the Population Registration Act, the Suppression of Communism Act, Group Areas Act, Bantu Authorities Act, and Separate Representation of (Coloured) Voters Act.

Nearly 10,000 volunteers of all races went to gaol for deliberately defying [these] six selected racially discriminatory laws. It was the biggest political demonstration ever seen in South Africa.

When, late in 1952, there was serious rioting in three Cape Province towns, where the Defiance Campaign had been particularly successful—Port Elizabeth, East London and Kimberley—White South Africa was shocked when the rioters murdered several White persons, among them a nun. [George Clay and Stanley Uys, *Africa South*][14]

African Defiance Campaign Extends to Natal

DURBAN, Monday: Non-European organisations last night extended their defiance campaign to Natal when 21 members of the African and Indian Congress—four of them women—were arrested for breaking the railway apartheid regulations at Durban's Berea railway station. Railway policemen with 21 prisoners had to force their way through a crowd of about 1,000 Africans and Indians who chanted "Afrika" and gave the thumbs-up — the sign of the movement. Among those arrested were Doctor G. M. Naicker, President of the Natal Indian Congress, and P. J. Simalene, Assistant Secretary of the African National Congress.

Defiers filed into a waiting room marked "Europeans Only," sat down and lit cigarettes. [*Inverell Times*, NSW][15]

PUBLIC SAFETY ACT, ACT NO 3 OF 1953

This act was passed in response to the ANC's civil disobedience campaigns in particular the **Defiance Campaign** of 1952, instigated by Nelson Mandela, Walter Sisulu, and other prominent members of the ANC. The Act empowered the government to declare stringent **states of emergency** and increased penalties for protesting against or supporting the repeal of a law.

Under a state of emergency, the Minister of Law and Order, the Commissioner of the South African Police (SAP), a magistrate, or a commissioned officer could detain any person for reasons of public safety. It further provided for the detention without trial for any dissent. [*Omics International*][16]

The Press and the Defiance Campaign   In May, 1952, Mr. Strijdom, then still Pretender to the Premiership, criticized the role of the English Press and warned it that newspaper editors had been flogged once in South Africa. "When the final Press law comes, it will give the Government power of life and death over not only *New Age,* but over all other newspapers."

Strijdom Keeps His Threat   As a direct consequence of the Defiance Campaign, the Nationalist Government introduced, at the short Parliamentary session in January, 1953, the "Terrible Twins": The Public Safety Act and the Criminal Laws Amendment Act, …which forbade, in fact, public expressions of sympathy with a defiance campaign.

"There are two evil spirits in South Africa and I name them: These princes of the church, these so-called churchmen, who have become nothing else but political agitators who openly preach rebellion. **The second evil spirit is the contemptible English Press** which stops at nothing, whether it is murder or crime or manslaughter or sabotage. Everything is grasped at with only one object, and that is to break this party which is the only bulwark in the whole continent of Africa." [J.C. Greyling, *Africa South*][17]

CHAPTER 5

MARKET DAY

I was excited when Mother let me accompany her to the market in the city. She didn't always want to take me. She hurried everywhere she went, and I suppose I dawdled along, fascinated by every sight and smell. She left home early in the morning, around five a.m., before the sun baked the town and lifted the heat off the pavement in shimmering waves. Her big, woven grass market basket was in the trunk of the car, (called the "boot" in British English). There were no supermarkets, just small neighborhood groceries called tea rooms. She could phone in an order to the local tea room, which sold an array of grocery items, and send Piet to pick it up, or it might be delivered to our house in the back of a jalopy. I can still hear her loud, carrying voice coming from the little room under the stairs where she sat when she telephoned. She had no idea her voice was so loud. Sometimes it was embarrassing, like the time we were in the elevator at a department store. There were several other people going up to the next floor with us when she announced in her infamous stage whisper, "We'll get your bras next."

There was an Indian Market, a Native Market, and an English Market in Durban. The big city markets carried items that the small local grocers didn't sell. Mother bought fresh fish and lettuce at the English Market, which was held indoors in a big building kept cool by a high ceiling. It was extremely clean, with shining glass counters lined up in rows, white ladies in starched white uniforms and caps wrapping Mother's choice of fresh-caught king clip or sole in clean, white paper. My brother Michael described the English Market as "boring." Indian vegetable growers used human waste, "night soil," as fertilizer in their fields, a practice that could spread serious disease. Pehr and Kirstin both contracted amoebic dysentery in spite of Mother's care in purchasing "clean" foods, so she always bought lettuce at the English Market, as well as any other vegetable that could carry particles of soil. And Dad grew lettuce in our garden, too. He loved to grow vegetables, wherever we lived. He grew lovely flowers, too.

Rachel and Michael shelling peas, Durban, South Africa, 1949

Dad once smuggled in a packet of Golden Bantam corn he'd bought on a trip to America. In South Africa corn was not grown to eat on the cob. Instead, it was ground into a meal and served as porridge, called mealie meal. Our cook, Miriam Nyandu, took care of the corn patch. We liked to hide in it as the green stalks grew higher, but we were warned that green mamba snakes like to hide in the corn, too. The British word for wheat is corn, while corn is called maize; the Afrikaans word for corn has its origin in Portuguese and has been anglicized to mealies, so it can get a little confusing in conversation.

Mother bought bananas from the Indian Market. When she had picked out a suitable-looking bunch, the seller would tell her, "Two shillings, Missus! Nice ripe bananas." Putting the bananas back in the carton, she would stalk away, and he would immediately call after her, insisting, "One and eight pence, Missus. Please. Just one and eight." She might turn back, hesitating, saying, "One and six." Eventually, she would prevail. She became a real artist at bargaining. There were twelve pennies in a shilling, and twenty shillings in a pound, which made elementary school arithmetic a nightmare. In 1970 South Africa adopted the metric system and the monetary system is now based on the Rand.

The Indian Market was chaotic and noisy, a cluttered, hodgepodge of stalls, with partitions made of woven grass or colorful fabric. Rickety tables and upturned barrels laden with baskets and cardboard boxes were piled high with fruits and other, often unrecognizable, edibles. Indians sold what were called sweetmeats, "coolie pink" gelatinous squares artfully arranged in pyramids. The word "coolie" was applied to Indians whenever criticism was intended, for example, "coolie busses" spewed foul exhaust. Drivers avoided getting stuck behind one of them in heavy traffic. Mother never let us try the sweetmeats, though their bright color beckoned to us from Indian shop windows as we drove through the Indian section of town. I don't know what they were made of, or why she wouldn't let us taste them, but they were probably delicious. Because of their use of human waste as fertilizer, there was at that time a distinct distrust among white citizens for anything Indians might cook. It was sure to carry germs of some kind. That was in the days before curry became a favored restaurant dish. Brass shops in the market displayed their shiny objects, crowded together, some hanging off the walls, next to small, neat spice shops with glass counters. The scent of exotic spices filled the humid air and mixed with the smell of discarded, overripe vegetables and trodden fruit made slippery by many feet, some with shoes, the majority without. Crowds of people working close together added to the unique aroma, which brewed and became more pungent as the day heated up.

On one trip to the Indian market Mother was searching for a particular rice-seller who had been recommended by a friend. Brown rice was then a precious commodity, and was not sold in grocery stores. She hoped she could find his stall, as there was no guarantee it would be just where her friend had said it would be. When she found the little shop that she believed was the right one, she told the man standing behind the counter what she wanted. He shook his head and said, "No, no, Missus, I don't have any brown rice. Never. Not at all." He rolled his "r" in "never." She peered down through the glass counter, her mouth screwed up, not believing him, and then, looking him in the eye, she asked again. Again, he replied that he didn't have any brown rice. She said she knew he had some, that a friend had told her he sold brown rice. "What's that in that brown paper bag?" she inquired, pointing. Reluctantly, he quickly weighed out what amounted to about a cup of rice, poured it into a small brown bag, folded down the top, and quoted an exorbitant price. She hesitated, treating him to a silent stare, almost a glare, and then paid it. That may have been the only time Dad enjoyed a meal with brown rice in South Africa.

She was equally firm with the butcher. She demanded a particular cut of "lean, streaky bacon," and once returned some lamb that she insisted was mutton, which is tough and cheaper than lamb.

The Native market was more lively. The Africans brought goats and chickens to sell at market along with fruits and vegetables. They must have brought everything on the train, all the way from the country. They didn't own trucks or cars, and getting a driver's license would have been impossible for Africans in those days. Mother looked for juicy lychees—the prickly-skinned fruit was sold in bunches, like grapes—and naartjies, the extra-sweet South African tangerines. She picked out tart green Granny Smith apples, and peaches, especially the sweet white-fleshed peaches from Alpha Farm in the Orange Free State.

Friends who were members of our church lived on Alpha Farm. We visited there sometimes, even though it was a long drive from Durban, about five hundred kilometers, the road running from Ladysmith through Van Reenen's Pass, to Harrismith, and on to Ladybrand in the Free State. Distance in such places must be judged by time. Even today, with modern paved roads, it's a seven to nine-hour drive.

Making ice cream with hailstones. Mother, Mike, Rachel …
Jeannette (with braids), Pehr standing at right, Alpha
Farm, Ladybrand, South Africa, 1950.

Alpha Farm ran alongside the Caledon River, which serves as the boundary between Lesotho and South Africa in that locality. Dad met with the Basuto ministers and members of their congregations there. In the dry season, they could just walk across the river on the stones because the water level was so low.

The peaches that grew at Alpha Farm were white-fleshed, tender and sweet. Because of their fragility, the crop could be completely ruined by a hail storm. One year when we were at the farm, the hail was so deep on the ground it looked like snow. We gathered it in buckets and made ice cream—using hailstones in place of ice—with one of those old fashioned, hand-cranked ice cream machines.

Group exploring Bushman cave near Alpha Farm. Dad with hat and walking stick, Ladybrand, South Africa, 1951

There were bushman caves in the mountains near Alpha decorated with San paintings from long, long ago. In one cave we picked up quartz crystals—geodes, pieces of round rocks with a hollow cavity lined with crystals—relics of ancient volcanic activity. We regarded the shiny crystals as treasures. They looked just like diamonds, sparkling in the sun.

Mother's market basket, Durban, South Africa

As Mother's basket grew heavy, filled with fresh fruit and vegetables, she would suddenly be surrounded by sharp-eyed, observant little Indian boys, each one "claiming" her, offering to carry her basket to the car: "Just sixpence, Madam. I'll take it for you." She usually allowed a boy to help her, but she had to follow carefully as he deftly darted in and out of the crowded marketplace like quicksilver. We arrived home in time for breakfast.

Shopping with Mother was never boring.

<hr />

NATIVES ABOLITION OF PASSES AND COORDINATION OF DOCUMENTS ACT, ACT NO 67 OF 1952

Commonly known as the Pass Laws, rather than abolishing the use of the pass book as the name would suggest, this ironically named law disposed of local passes and made it compulsory for all Black South Africans—male or female—over the age of 16 to carry a central government issued pass book at all times.

A pass included a photograph, details of place of origin, employment record, tax payments, and encounters with the police. It was a criminal offence to be unable to produce a pass when required to do so by the police. No black person could leave a rural area for an urban one without a permit from the local authorities. On arrival in an urban area a permit to seek work had to be obtained within 72 hours.

PASSES AND AFRICANS   PASS! No other word in the country conjures up such a variety of associations as this one word … To the African it rouses memories of police raids, of members of families estranged from one another, of children separated from parents, of fathers sent to serve terms of imprisonment, and of humiliation in its bitterest form … And cases are on record in which policemen have arrested women under curfew regulations and abused them. If women have to carry passes which must be produced on demand … thousands of African women are thus going to be arrested by male policemen and the number of abuses increased commensurately. [W.B. Ngakane, *The Black Sash*][18]

INTERVIEW WITH DAN TLOOME
I was particularly… touched, you know, by the pass laws … how people were being arrested, you know, in great numbers every day—they are taken to the commissioner, what they called at the time Native Commissioner's Court … in a month's time hundreds of people will be taken away from town, Johannesburg, to go and work in the farms because they had no—they were told their passes were out of order and the taxes were out of order…

Now what really touched me [most] of all was a certain farm where these people were told to go and dig potatoes, you know, [with] their nails, their fingers, and so on—I'm forgetting what the place was, but ... all the people who were fined ... in the magistrates' court, used to be taken to these farms to go and work for the farmers without pay.

[Dan Tloome, *Digital Innovation South Africa*][19]

CHAPTER 6

THE AFRICAN MINISTERS

My father worked with two groups of African theological students. One group of men lived in the province of Natal, many of them from the area then called Zululand, now KwaZulu Natal. The other group lived in Lesotho, which was called Basutoland, an independent country completely surrounded by South Africa. Basutoland was a Protectorate of the British Crown, like Bechuanaland, which is now known as Botswana. These two countries were never under the rule of the South African government. The theological students met together for classes in theology and the languages of the Old and New Testaments, Hebrew and Greek. They were also expected to learn Latin because Swedenborg's theological works were written in Latin. While these books have been translated into many European languages, only a few have been translated into African languages.

There was a small seat in the kitchen at 185 Sydenham Road, a triangle of white painted wood, wedged into the corner, barely wide enough to sit on. One winter day, Rev. Nelson Gcabashe came into the kitchen to get warm after walking from the bus stop. Nelson was always smiling and friendly. His suit jacket was buttoned tightly over his knitted vest. He had travelled a long way from his home in Ndwedwe, some fifty-seven kilometers north of Durban. He had to take several different busses to get to our house. It took a lot of time. As he settled himself into the corner seat he greeted our cook, Miriam, who was busy peeling potatoes at one end of the big old wooden kitchen table. She used a paring knife, preferring it to the potato peeler mother used. She offered to make him a cup of tea, which he gratefully accepted, wrapping his hands around the chipped enameled tin cup. Nelson smiled as the warmth spread into his cold fingers. He had a wide smile, in spite of his missing teeth:

"Aheh, Ngiyabonga," "Thank you," he said.

We children loved Miriam. She was plump and grandmotherly and kind. Mike says she willingly cooked several kinds of hot cereal for breakfast because we were all so fussy—we didn't like Dad's Tiger Oats. She wore a blue cotton dress and white apron, with a white "doek," or scarf, on her head. On Sundays she dressed very smartly for church, exchanging her white head scarf for a soft velvet hat. We liked to watch her work with a sharp knife because she had a peculiar thumb, missing the last joint, and what remained of the thumb nail was misshapen, like a dried-up currant. It was amazing what she could do with that thumb. I don't remember that she ever told anyone how it came to be injured. Perhaps she was born with it? Miriam had some strong opinions. We had a pot with a dented bottom that wouldn't sit flat on the stove. She called it the "ama-Pondo" pot. Anything that didn't work right or was broken she described that way, quietly muttering under her breath. The Pondos were a Xhosa-speaking tribe that lived south of Durban in an area that became known as the Transkei. As far as Miriam was concerned, nothing good came from them, they didn't measure up to proud Zulu standards. The Transkei was destined to become one of the first Bantustans, a reserve for separate development.

Mother grew to know the theological students well. She cared greatly about their families and enjoyed teaching them Hebrew. Her artistic ability was a benefit when it came to drawing Hebrew letters. She had special pens and ink to work with. When she heard Nelson's voice, Mother joined us in the kitchen. She greeted him in Zulu, *Sawubona!* Holding out her hands to grasp both of his, she asked him how his wife, Florence was feeling. Florence suffered from African sleeping sickness, *Trypanosomiasis*, a serious parasitic disease acquired from the bite of a tsetse fly. Tsetse flies were common in areas to the north of us, where they are monitored and controlled by dipping cattle in in-secticide. When we travelled to beautiful Saint Lucia's Bay, the car was sprayed with insecticide as we exited the park. Another parasitic illness we were warned about was bilharzia, or *schistosomiasis*. The organisms are found in snails that live in freshwater lakes and streams and enter the body through the urinary tract or the intestines.

Malaria was controlled by strict rules about standing water. There were no screens on windows or doors. If you saw a mosquito, the city would send someone to inspect your house and yard for poorly drain-ing gutters or flower pots collecting rain water. We had an insecticide sprayer with DDT in it. Mike and I used to chase each other around, squirting DDT at the escaping victim. But we also played with balls of mercury from broken glass thermometers, rolling the little silver balls around in the palms of our hands.

Mother sometimes drove Florence Gcabashe for treatment at the Zulu McCord's Hospital, the only hospital in Durban that accepted Af-rican patients. Florence and Nelson had a large family. They gave their children names like Duke and Princess. They all sang together, beautiful-ly. White church members, who noticed that Mother allowed Florence to ride in the front seat of the car, scolded her: "You shouldn't do that. It gives them ideas!" they warned. My father was similarly scolded for allowing the African ministers to use his office telephone. It was custom-ary to keep a little tin coin box by the telephone. Guests were expected to drop a three penny bit, a silver "tickey," (thruppence or three-pence), into the box when they made a telephone call. The African ministers did the same. My father and mother just ignored the scolds.

At the start of my father's work in South Africa, the theological students met in his study, a converted double garage. The Zulu stu-dents travelled to Durban on busses from their segregated townships. None of them would have had a car. To teach the Basuto students, he drove all the way to Lesotho. Later on, they could all come together for classes at the hostel the church built in Mayville. Dad's study was a good-sized room, with a big table in the center where the students gathered. One wall was covered with bookcases. He kept the books he most often referred to when writing a sermon in a revolving bookcase by his desk, books like concordances and Latin dictionaries.

Dad's study after garage renovation, Durban, South Africa, 1950

Siri and safe with Swedenborg First editions,
Durban, South Africa, 1955

Next to the wall by his desk was a safe, a heavy, green metal box on legs, where he kept copies of first editions of Swedenborg's works. Published in the eighteenth century, the books were all written in Latin, the language of science and philosophy, rather than in Swedenborg's native language, Swedish. Dad was a fluent Latin scholar. He could stand at the lectern in a church service and translate straight into English while reading in Latin. With its humid climate, Durban was not a good place to store rare books. But the original editions, as he always referred to them, were very important to him. I assume he didn't want to leave them in America in case he never returned.

Emanuel Swedenborg (1688-1772) was a brilliant Swedish scientist, engineer, inventor, and philosopher. He turned to theology after experiencing a spiritual awakening in his mid-fifties. In his many writings he lays down the relationship between the spiritual and physical worlds. Drawing from the Bible, reasoning, and his own spiritual experiences, Swedenborg wrote at length about the nature of God and the human mind; the spiritual world and the life after death; and the path to salvation. For example, in the twelve volumes of the *Arcana Coelestia*, or *Heavenly Secrets*, he uncovers the inner meaning of the story of Creation as describing the steps to a person's spiritual regeneration.[20] His works have been translated into many languages, worldwide, but they were originally published in Holland and England because their content would have been considered in opposition to the Swedish state religion, the Lutheran Church. One of my father's Swedish ancestors—many of whom believed in Swedenborg's revelation—daringly disseminated his teachings from his Lutheran pulpit.

Only Whites were allowed to worship in the church in Durban where Dad preached to his congregation on Sunday mornings. If the African ministers were invited to attend a special service, they needed permission from the authorities. They would then sit and listen on the porch outside the open windows—in order not to offend the white parishioners. I can remember only one time when they came into the church, seated in the back row, and that was when my brother Pehr was ordained into the priesthood. I was too young to know whether any of those white people, "Europeans," would have agreed with us about the mistreatment of blacks in South Africa. I don't think so. One woman I know said she had never been into her servants' kaias. She claimed that she treated them well, but was apparently unaware of the deplorable state of the living quarters she provided. Another woman, serving salad at the dinner table, scolded her cook harshly, in front of her guests, for not cutting the cucumber thinly enough. My sister knew of a neighbor who would not let her "girl" go home for a week to see her family upcountry. She said she would just get another girl if that one took off on a holiday. Jeannette herself allowed her servant to bring her daughter to stay in her kaia during the child's school holidays, even though this was illegal.

Such was the culture of apartheid that in 1950 the government issued a policy that prohibited non-whites from living, working, or even entering the city without documentation. The Group Areas Act dictated where people of the different races could live. Whites, Africans, Coloureds (mixed-raced), and Indians, were assigned to different residential zones. Non-whites could not live or work or visit within the city without their identity book, the hated passbook, stamped with the name and address of their employer. If they were caught without their pass, they were arrested.

Mayville Hostel, opening day, Durban, South Africa, 1951

When the African theological students were no longer allowed to meet in Dad's office, the church purchased some land in Mayville, in an area zoned for black people. One side of the property faced a row of Indian shacks. The Indians cooked their meals outside on open fires. In addition to the food odors, there were the sounds of cackling chickens and barking dogs, but Dad just had to put up with it. Cato Manor, the notoriously crowded and dangerous black township was situated on the other side of the hill from the hostel. One day, in a protest march, the residents of Cato Manor walked all the way to City Hall. They were making a "trilling" sound but were not acting in an aggressive manner. However, when she heard about the streams of Africans walking through the Mayville property, mother quickly took the car and went to fetch our father. The government was always warning us about impending bloodbaths if the Africans were to rise against us.

The hostel was arranged with a number of bedrooms opening onto a veranda. The kitchen and dining room were at one end. A large corrugated iron building at the other end was divided into a classroom and church sanctuary. Students could stay and study for a period of weeks at a time, making it much easier for the men who travelled a long way from rural areas of Natal or from Lesotho. The cook, an old man named Tom, had only a few white tufts of hair on top of his head. Mother thought he must be at least one hundred years old because elderly Zulus don't usually have white hair. He had to prepare the preferred foods for both Zulus and Basutos to keep everybody happy.

On the occasions when Dad preached in the church in Mayville, Rev. Benjamin Ngiba translated the sermons into Zulu for the congregation. Rev. Ngiba had graduated from college in Durban in the years before the apartheid government barred black Africans from pursuing higher education via the Bantu Education Act. He was so completely attuned to my father's theological thinking that he would start translating before Dad even finished a sentence. An accomplished pianist, Rev. Ngiba would then sit down at the piano and accompany the hymns. He was a very dignified man.

Rev. Benjamin Ngiba, Durban, South Africa, 1959

Mother sewed the ministers' white linen robes from scratch. There was an inner robe and an outer robe. She consulted with a seamstress, Mrs. Defty, an instructor at the Natal Technical College in Durban, who helped her make patterns to fit each man according to his measurements, which she carefully recorded in a big notebook with diagrams. One gentleman had a particularly big neck. She struggled with the pattern, and when she thought she'd "got it just right," it still didn't fit him the way she wanted. The white linen was expensive, and Mother never did like mathematics, so it must have been with great trepidation that she took that first cut into the material. She went to the Indian fabric bazaars to purchase the linen. There were rows of such shops on Berea Road in Durban, stuffed with bolts of every kind of material: colorful silk for saris; heavier fabric for drapery and slipcovers; and bright cottons in every color, piled high on tables and on shelves going up the walls.

She sewed the ministers' robes on the electric Wilcox & Gibbs sewing machine she'd brought from America. She made dresses for us, too, and we girls all learned how to sew on that machine. She laid out her work on the big dining table. At the end of each day, in time to set the table for dinner, she would fold up her work, pins, paper patterns, and tape measure, and put it all away carefully in the big linen press in the dining room. The advantage of that particular sewing machine, the Wilcox & Gibbs, she said, was that it sewed with a chain stitch, which made it very easy to pull out the stitches of a seam, unlike the lock stitch Singer sewing machine that pulls the thread up from underneath with a bobbin mechanism. I probably shouldn't tell this little story about the life of one robe, so I'll omit the minister's name: on a return trip to South Africa, after said reverend gentleman had passed away, it was noticed that the table covering in his family's house was of interestingly-shaped fine white linen.

There were several rural African church congregations in the province of Natal. Rev. Paul Buthelezi lived in the Bergville district, a rural area not too far from the mountains where we enjoyed our holidays. Rev. Buthelezi's compound was neat and tidy, the ground swept bare, the doors and wooden window frames painted red or blue, in contrast to the dark brown of the mud-plastered walls and thatched roofs. He and his wife Irene lived there with their extended family. Because of its proximity to our vacation house in the Berg, we once attended a church service at Rev. Buthelezi's place in Bergville.

It was the custom among the Zulus for important guests to sit in front of the altar, facing the congregation, usually on some kind of platform. Michael, Siri, and I were uncomfortable sitting up front that way, where everyone could look at us. Ministers' families usually have to sit in the front row because everybody else avoids it, but at least at home we sat facing the altar and not the congregation. There were a lot of distractions: Mothers fed their babies at the breast (something I'd never seen), and a chicken jumped up onto the altar, clucking loudly. The women tried to shoo the flapping bird out of the church, which was quickly becoming stiflingly hot. Halfway through the service, the children were excused—a sermon or a communion service was considered too long and complicated for children to sit still for—so we went out to wait in the car. Thankfully, it had been parked in the shade.

Rachel Longstaff. Rev. Buthelezi's house. Mrs. Irene Buthelezi and Alan Longstaff sitting outside in sun, Bergville, KwaZulu Natal, 1990

We were immediately surrounded by a horde of excited children, clamoring in Zulu, knocking and banging on the car windows. We had never before encountered a crowd of people, of any age or race, pointing and calling out to us like that. They were just being friendly, but it startled us. When a group of teenaged girls offered us steaming mugs of strong hot tea diluted with plenty of sweetened condensed milk, I'm glad we were polite enough to open the car windows and accept it.

I have deep regrets about that experience. I wish we had been prepared for it, that there had been more contact between the white members of the church and the African membership. It would have been enriching to interact with those children, to play a game, or just laugh or sing with them, never mind the language barrier. Why weren't we taught to speak Zulu in school? Instead, we learned Afrikaans, "the language of the oppressor." And something in our environment had taught us to be wary, even afraid, of black Africans.

Photographer unknown. Pehr on horseback. Note
Basuto pony, Senqunyane, Lesotho, 1961

The most remote church group was in Senqunyane, in Basu-toland,[21] far up in the Malutis, the mountain range that forms that country's eastern border with South Africa. It could be reached only on horseback. Pehr, who loved hiking and riding horseback in the mountains, delighted in visiting Senqunyane—the "q" in Senqunyane is pronounced as a click. I doubt very much if my father ever went there. He was afraid of horses, something we teased him about because his name, Philip, means "lover of horses" in Greek.

Recognizing the importance of both secular and religious education to the church membership in Lesotho, Mother sponsored one of the minister's wives, Mrs. Evodia Mphatse, making it possible for her to obtain a teacher's certificate. She attended teachers' college in Maseru, Lesotho, where she was awarded a diploma in Education. The church built a school, *The Lord's New Church Primary School*, in Khopane, Lesotho, on the grounds of the church building where her husband, the late Rev. Gershon Mphatse, was pastor. Evodia served as principal teacher for many years and was much loved by the pupils.

Church Primary School. Rev. Gershon Mphatse and
Mrs. Evodia Mphatse, Khopane, Lesotho, 1959

One of the Basuto ministers, the elderly and dignified Rev. Twentyman Mofokeng, once travelled to Durban to participate in a session at the theological school. One day someone telephoned our house from the hostel in Mayville, where he was staying. He said they were worried about Rev. Mofokeng. As Dad was not home, Mother went in his place, and she took me with her as she didn't leave us alone in the house when we were small. He was lying on his back outside on the veranda. Mother knelt beside him, holding a mirror in front of his face. She stood up after a few minutes, slowly shaking her head. The small group of people standing with her had been trying to decide if he was still alive. They bowed their heads and someone gently folded Rev. Mofokeng's hands over his chest.

Photographer unknown. Church group in Lesotho 1939. Dad, Mother in center front

I had never seen a dead person. She insists that I couldn't have seen the body; she thought I was sitting in the car the whole time. But I must have followed her, so I did see him. He was a big man with broad shoulders and a distinguished face. As is the custom in his homeland, hundreds of mourners would accompany Rev. Mofokeng's coffin, walking through the fields and over the hills, singing hymns as they made their way to the gravesite. It is a moving and beautiful way to see someone off to the next world.

Rev. Mofokeng and Rev. Tlali both came from Lesotho. Rev. Mofokeng was a tall man, but Rev. Tlali was very small, with a sad face Dad described as "droopy." When Rev. Tlali's wife was accused of witchcraft, it meant he could no longer serve the church as a minister, according to the Basuto church leader, in spite of the fact that the district judge pointed out that Rev. Tlali was not the one being accused of witchcraft.

Two of the Zulu ministers had the last name Jiyana. Mother told us that the Jiyana family had been "Praisers to the King" (King of the Zulus) in the past. The African ministers were referred to by their surnames, such as "Ngiba," for Rev. Benjamin Ngiba, instead of "Benjamin," as house servants would have been addressed—except when they were referred to as "boy." The Zulus address ministers as "Umfundisi," meaning pastor, or teacher. Dad required the ministers to wear suits and ties, and dress shoes, as he did himself, which gave them a degree of respectability not shared by male house servants, who wore uniform white cotton short pants and loose short-sleeved shirts, plain but cool for working in that warm climate.

Our family remembers the African ministers with great affection. They worked under extremely difficult circumstances, in dangerous times, ever loyal to my father and to the church. They were respected and beloved by their congregations. Some years later, on a visit to Lesotho, one of the Basuto ministers' wives greeted me with the African handshake, and said to me, "You are an African."

"I am honored," I replied.

BILLY KHOZA, DAD'S SECRETARY

A smaller office adjoining Dad's was for his secretary, Billy Khoza. There was a door that opened out back to the area where Piet's kaia was. Billy, as an African, was supposed to enter the office from the back. He was also supposed to use the servants' bathroom, but he used to come into the house and use the toilet by the back door instead. I'm sure the white church members would have been scandalized if they had known, but my parents said nothing.

One of Billy's duties was to type my father's sermons onto a stencil, a wax-coated paper form that he fitted onto an inked Gestetner copying machine. By turning the handle, ink was pressed through the holes made by the typewriter keys. My mother proofread the first copy. Mother was an expert in English and spelling. She told us she'd learned from a good teacher in school. In addition, her father, editor of *New Church Life*, had her proofread the magazine with him by reading every word in each paragraph backwards, from last word to first. When Mother discovered an error in Billy's typing, he would paint over the offending letter with pink correction fluid that smelled like nail polish, and the stencil was re-inserted into the typewriter. It was hard to get that new letter to go in just the right place. When the copies started getting too light, he added more ink to the machine. This was a messy job, but we liked the strong inky smell that filled the room and Billy sometimes let us turn the handle.

Jeannette on swing. Door to Billy's office in back, Durban, South Africa, 1956

Billy was very patient with us children. When we were about seven years old, a school friend and I decided to write stories for teaching younger children to read. We asked if we could please use Billy's typewriter, but Dad replied that it was "up to Billy." With Billy's permission, we spent a number of Saturday mornings sitting at the typing table in the corner of his office, typing our little books and illustrating them with colored pencils.

Between 1948 and 1994 South Africa was a veritable police state. The South African secret police, Special Branch, were menacing and wielded a lot of power. One morning at about three a.m., there was a loud pounding on our front door. It was the secret police, demanding access to Dad's office. They informed him that Billy Khoza was a member of the African National Congress, or ANC, and they then proceeded to look through Dad's desk and his papers to determine whether he, too, was an active supporter of the banned political movement. Most of the Zulu ministers in our church belonged to Inkatha, the political party of the ethnic Zulus, but one of them was a member of the ANC, an organization branded as "Communist" by the South African government. At a time when distrust between members of the two political parties sometimes erupted into murderous violence, in Durban and elsewhere, my father asked his students not to discuss politics. He emphasized that the church must remain apolitical, so the discovery that Billy was an ANC member was a problem for him. The church must remain "below the radar," or we risked being deported.

In spite of this, Jeannette remembers being present at a clandestine midnight meeting, where Dad and Billy quietly helped someone who was trying to escape from South Africa. Dad reluctantly decided he would have to fire Billy, and Mother took over the job of typing sermons.

Billy eventually became a successful businessman and store-owner. When one of his daughters was attending college in the U.S., he and his wife visited my parents in their Philadelphia home. My mother served them tea. It was a moment of sweet irony.

Mayville. African ministers and Odhner family
farewell group, Durban, South Africa, 1960

APARTHEID AND THE CHURCH

Report of the Church Commission of the Study Project on Christianity in Apartheid Society regarding the effects of apartheid on the Church in South Africa
The South African Council of Churches and the Christian Institute of Southern Africa, are joint sponsors of SPRO-CAS.

(Excerpts)

In terms of the "Church Clause" of the **Native Laws Amendment Act** of 1957, Africans may be prevented from attending Church Services in the "white" part of a town by order of the Minister with the concurrence of the local authority if in their opinion they are causing a nuisance or if it is undesirable for them to be present from the point of view of their numbers. It appears necessary for a complaint to be received for this clause to be applied.

The restriction against Whites, Coloured people and Asiatics visiting African areas, whether township or rural, without special permits ... also makes it difficult for laymen from those racial groups to worship or meet together with African congregations.

A Church with white members but a black majority faces much difficulty in acquiring or holding property in "white" areas. As most Churches in South Africa, unless racially divided, have a black majority, this makes it extremely difficult for them to be accurately registered as a white body. However, if such a Church refuses to be inaccurately [sic] registered it encounters this pressing problem regarding property.

Church sites are granted in some "white" areas only on condition that the trustees guarantee that no one who is not white will be allowed to attend church activities on it. [emphasis mine]

Religious workers from countries outside the Republic coming to this country to be employed by the Church require a permit which is granted for a period of 12 months, and which may be renewed for a further period thereafter. In cases where the government does not deem it desirable to renew a permit, the application for extension is refused. After three to five years, application may be made for permanent residence and if this is granted the need for a permit then ceases. However, the granting of permanent residence can be rescinded, with no reasons given and no right of appeal. In this way a number of clergy have already been served with deportation orders.

Church workers from foreign countries are inhibited owing to the knowledge that their right to remain in, or return to, this country may not be renewed if the government takes exception to anything they say.

Banning is another action the Government may take, and is increasingly taking against clergy and other church workers (for example, Father Cosmas Desmond, Rev. Stanley Ntwasa, Rev. Basil Moore, Mr. David de Beer). The fear of losing one's passport or being banned inhibits criticism of the government's policy.

Recent government actions (July, 1972) include the banning of the Rev. S. Hayes and the withdrawal of the passport of Mr. Peter Randall, the director of SPRO-CAS.

[Peter Randall, *Digital Innovation South Africa*][22]

CHAPTER 7

OUR FRIEND VICTOR

Victor was in a hurry. He needed to get home before dark. It gets dark suddenly in the tropics, around five o'clock. There is no long, light-lingering evening with blinking fireflies for children in Africa to enjoy. Victor pushed the metal ring in front of him with a long, thin stick, his bare feet making no sound as he ran behind it along the sidewalk. The wheel rattled along the pavement as he ran faster. Lots of young African boys (then often referred to as "piccanins") made toys from pieces of discarded metal like the rims of bicycle tires. Victor steered it carefully so it wouldn't fall or roll down off the curb into the street.

Victor lived with Miriam, his grandmother—our cook and kitchen maid—in a kaia in the back yard of our house. He had left his family in the country and come to town to attend school. He wasn't allowed to attend a "white" school, but there were better schools for African children in the city in those days. Rural schools had no books, or desks, or chairs. Many of those schools still, today, lack the things we take for granted in a school.

Miriam Nyandu, our cook and Victor's grandmother,
Durban, South Africa, 1954

Miriam's kaia was small and dark, with a single window and a door. It smelled musty, especially when it rained. There was a bed for each of them, and a small table. The only light came from the dim globe in the ceiling. Victor rarely came into our house, and then not past the kitchen, where he sometimes sat to get warm. On those occasions he kept very quiet. He never went upstairs into our bedrooms, and we never shared a meal with him. Miriam had taught him the rules. It was just the way it was. Nobody asked questions. We took it for granted. We were taught to respect the privacy of the servants' rooms, so we didn't visit Victor in the kaia, either.

Victor and Miriam didn't eat the same kind of food we ate, except for chicken. She carried the food she had cooked out to the kaia on white enameled metal plates. Some of them had chipped blue rims. They ate samp (crushed corn), madumbes (a hairy-skinned, potato-like carbohydrate), and sometimes a green leafy vegetable she called spinach, which she picked from weeds in the back of the garden. Dad complained about the smell of the greens when they were cooking—it wafted up through the whole house, he said. Mother let Miriam go ahead and cook the greens, concerned that they ate such a carbohydrate-heavy diet. They needed some vegetables, she would have argued. Dad could air out the house, one of his many eccentricities. He even did that in below-freezing cold weather in Pennsylvania.

We liked to play with Victor. He and Michael were about the same age: ten or twelve years old at the time Victor was living at 185 Sydenham Road. Victor's life was very different from ours. He never had the opportunity to go to the beach or visit a library or a museum. He had no toys other than what he could create with his own hands from bits and pieces, like the old bike tire rim. Mike remembers that Victor played a much more challenging game of hopscotch than we did—you had to balance a stone on your head as you hopped. Try it: it's very hard to keep that stone in place. The two of them climbed the big old avocado tree that grew out of the chicken coop. From there, they could jump onto the flat roof of that garage where all sorts of junk was kept.

*Front lawn. Mother, Siri, Rachel, Kirstin, and
Jeannette, Durban, South Africa, 1953*

Siri and I once joined Victor and Mike for a game of leapfrog on the front lawn. A sunny expanse, the front lawn was bounded by flower beds. Mother planted Barberton Daisies (African Daisy) and poinsettia bushes along the inside of the wall that paralleled Sydenham Road; pink and deep lavender cineraria grew in the shade of the avocado tree along the side of the driveway. The air smelled of warm grass, inviting us to play. We laughed together, tumbling about on the grass, chewing on the juicy ends of the grass stalks we pulled up. We liked to play a game where you put grass stalks into someone's mouth, the seeded ends sticking out on either side, saying it was a mustache. Then we would say a silly rhyme and pull the grass by the stalk ends, leaving the poor victim with a mouthful of grass seeds.

Siri's light cotton dress billowed up behind her like a sail as we played leapfrog. We were having a good time, until Mother came and told us to go play in the back yard, "behind the fence," she emphasized. We were "disturbing the ladies in the flats across the road," she said. They had telephoned her.

She didn't tell us right away, but they had complained because we were touching each other. We had thought we were just being too noisy. She mentioned the incident at the supper table, not wanting to discuss it in front of Victor. "It is inappropriate for black boys to touch white girls," the neighbors had told her. Mother was not comfortable with the idea that we were being spied on. "Perhaps they had nothing else to do," she said, "poor old things." Mother always tried to look for the good in people.

We have since learned that Victor went to medical school in another country and became a doctor. I truly hope he has found a fulfilling, new life, even if it has meant giving up his homeland.

<hr />

THE BANTU EDUCATION ACT, ACT NO 47 OF 1953
(Later renamed the Black Education Act, 1953)

Established a Black Education Department in the Department of Native Affairs which would compile a curriculum that suited the "nature and requirements of the black people." The pupils would be taught their Bantu cultural heritage and would be trained "in accordance with their opportunities in life," which he considered did not reach "above the level of certain forms of labour." [Hendrik Verwoerd, then Minister of Education]

The Act also removed state subsidies from denominational schools with the result that most of the mission-run African institutions were sold to the government or closed.

In 1953 the government passed the Bantu Education Act, which the people didn't want. We didn't want this bad education for our children. This Bantu Education Act was to make sure that our children only learnt things that would make them good for what the government wanted: to work in the factories and so on; they must not learn properly at school like the white children. Our children were to go to school only three hours a day, two shifts of children every day, one in the morning and one in the afternoon, so that more children could get a little bit of learning without government having to spend more money. Hawu! It was a terrible thing that act. [Frances Baard and Barbie Schreiner, *South African History Online*][23]

The Meaning of Bantu Education
The Director of Education of the Transvaal made it very clear that to "teach the Native to work" was the "true principle by which the education of the Native is to be regulated and controlled" and that a plan for "Native education" must "contemplate the ultimate social place of the native as an efficient worker."

The intensification of oppression and exploitation is extended to the teachers. Women teachers who are less expensive than men will be preferred. [Duma Nokwe, *Liberation*][24]

CHAPTER 8

PIET: GREEN MOLD AND DEAD RATS

Green mold grew on our black leather school shoes overnight. We kept them on the floor of our closed bedroom wardrobes, which may have made the problem worse. With the exception of military personnel and businessmen, most people in America today don't care whether their shoes are perfectly clean and shiny, especially schoolchildren's shoes. It was different in South Africa, maybe because there were people to polish them for us.

Piet Mkhize took care of all of our shoes. Light-skinned, Piet was slight of body, he looked as if he may have had some Bushman blood. He squatted in the corner of the hallway outside the kitchen with his brushes and polishing rags and little tins of black and brown shoe polish neatly lined up on the floor. He placed the shined shoes in a half circle in front of him. That careful placement of our shoes, in a half circle, must have been one way he could express his creativity.

Jeannette and Rachel setting off for school. Piet Mkhize in background, Durban, South Africa, 1954

That was only one of his jobs. On Sunday mornings, he put out the cups for after-church tea. They were pretty cups, cream-colored on the outside and pastel on the inside, with matching pastel saucers. I once complained to Mother that Piet did it all wrong—he mixed the colors, not matching cup to saucer. Mother said it should be my job from then on. I think that was unkind of me. He may have enjoyed the mismatched colors.

Piet was also responsible for polishing the big brass tray on the mantelpiece in the dining room. It was time-consuming, exacting work to remove the tarnish from all the little cracks. The tray had Hebrew letters in a circle around the edge and was embossed with mysterious figures. It had been in our grandparents' living room in Bryn Athyn, Pennsylvania. Mother and Dad, who had studied Biblical Hebrew in college, fell in love with each other while deciphering the words on that tray. It sat on the mantelpiece in every house we lived in. Since our parents passed away, none of us remembers what the words mean. Only recently my sister found someone to translate it for us. She discovered it is a Mizrach plate. The rabbi told her he believes it is from the Middle Eastern Mystical Jewish tradition. "Mizrach" means East in Hebrew, and Jews hang these pictures or platters in their homes on the east wall because that is the direction they face to pray. He was able to explain most of the people and symbols pictured on the tray. We don't know how our grandparents gained possession of it, though Grandfather Caldwell's passport was stamped with a visa for Palestine in April, 1925, issued by the British Consular General in Philadelphia.

On hot days Piet enjoyed standing with the hose, sprinkling the flowers in Dad's flower borders to keep them from wilting. Sometimes he carried on a conversation with a passing friend out on the sidewalk while he stood there in the cooling mist from the hose. He was also responsible for rolling the clay tennis court with the heavy iron roller filled with water, and he polished the floor of the church. Mother said he used too much polish—she complained that she could scrape it up off the floor with her fingernail.

The worst thing Piet was ever asked to do (or perhaps he volunteered to do it?) was to crawl into the space under the house to find a dead rat. A strong unpleasant odor had seeped up into a corner of the dining room one day, and a dead rat was the immediate assumption. There were no basements or cellars in South African houses, just crawl spaces, inhabited by huge spiders, definitely cockroaches, and the rats.

Chasing rats was something the men did together. Dad, Pehr, Mike, and Piet once chased a rat around the dining room with brooms. Through the closed doors we heard great shouts that sounded like fans at an athletic competition. I think Piet enjoyed being included in the mêlée, which is why I think he may have thought up the idea of going down under the house himself. He looked triumphant when he emerged with that dead rat, which he buried somewhere in the garden. There was another incident that Siri remembers about a rat that ran across the living room floor while we were having family worship after dinner. Pehr got up and chased after it, but it ran faster and hid in the closet under the stairs. Nobody wanted to go into the closet after that, but we kept our board games on the shelves in there, so we had to overcome our discomfort.

Piet lived in a kaia at the back of Dad's study. Mother and Dad were strict—we weren't allowed to go back there. Piet smoked dagga (marijuana). He grew his own plants in a weedy patch at the very back of our yard by the tennis court, where he hoped nobody would notice. One day the police came and searched the property. They found the dagga plants, and showed them to Dad. I don't think anyone was punished, but they all received a stern warning.

Piet had nothing to do for entertainment in his time off other than meet with friends, smoke dagga, or drink the homemade African beer called shimmeyaan. It was illegal to make shimmeyaan, brewed solely by African women. Black Africans were not allowed to attend movies, or concerts, or sporting events. There was only one beach they could visit, where Zulu women from upcountry filled empty Coke bottles with seawater and took it home to share with relatives on the farm. They believed seawater contained medicinal qualities. Perhaps the minerals in the seawater were missing from the soil where they planted their food crops?

Piet's life was particularly hard because he was classified as "Coloured," as one of his parents or grandparents was white. He had freckles, just like ours. Of mixed race, he was unacceptable in white society, probably not welcomed by black people, either. We knew almost nothing about him. He was very shy, didn't want his photo taken, and didn't talk to us about everyday things like family. Miriam, our cook, prepared his meals, and she would let Mother know if Piet was sick. Otherwise, he was very much in the background. But he was dependable. And he was predictable.

If African servants were out after curfew, or seen to be obviously inebriated, they were picked up by the police, beaten, and jailed overnight. When Mother was called to fetch Piet at the jail on Monday mornings, she was required to pay ten shillings in bail. One such day stands out in my memory: Piet was sitting in the corner seat in the kitchen, Mother hovering over him with a basin of water and a washcloth. His cheeks were so swollen from a beating the night before that they had actually split. Mother gently washed off the blood and gave him a cold compress to hold over his face.

Piet was important to our family.

———⟫✦⟪———

Separate Representation of Voters Act, Act No 46 of 1951

To make provision for the separate representation in Parliament and in the provincial council of the province of the Cape of Good Hope of Europeans and non-Europeans. Together with the 1956 amendment, this act led to the removal of Coloureds from the common voters' roll.

The Act had been invalidated by a decision of the South African courts as being unconstitutional.

The anger of many of the white voters of South Africa had been aroused by the government's proposal to enlarge the Senate, the upper House of Parliament, in order to ensure the two-thirds majority of both Houses required to remove the common roll voting rights of Coloured men. [Helen Joseph, *Tomorrow's Sun*][25]

OUR COLOURED PEOPLE
Recently we had the pathetic but perfectly appalling little spectacle of thirty Coloured children being either turned away or ejected from a City Theatre — Who in all that packed theatre would have taken offence at those thirty children sitting there, glued to their seats, gazing enraptured at the stage? (And if anyone *had* taken offence, surely he, and only he, the offended one, should have been ejected on the spot.)

I, as an Afrikaner, not unproud of our Afrikaner past and not unproud of our Huguenot and Protestant heritage, must repudiate our Prime Minister where some days ago he declared with great emphasis that our *Coloured people being, as they are, a minority, must be sacrificed to the good of the majority.* How strange to speak of our Coloured people as a minority when they comprise a group almost as big as we Afrikaners, when it will not be long before they are as many as we are ... and when here in Cape Town itself and in all the Peninsula they form the majority of our citizens! And it was not so long ago, too, that our Prime Minister laid down very firmly, very categorically, that our 1,500,000 Coloureds would never form part of the real, the true South African people. And this despite Dr. Donges recent assertion that five million hearts were now beating as one! [Uys Krige, *The Black Sash*][26]

[Note: For a discussion of the origins of the Coloured people of South Africa, please see the APPENDIX.]

CHAPTER 9

TENNIS WHITES

Competitors must be dressed in suitable tennis attire that is almost entirely white and this applies from the point at which the player enters the court surround. Shoes must be almost entirely white, including the soles.[27]

I was surprised and amused when I read a recent article in the *New York Times* about required tennis wear for Wimbledon contestants. I had no idea it was still such an important part of British tennis protocol.

When we moved into the house on Sydenham road in 1949, there was an old clay tennis court in our back yard with a tree growing in the middle of it. Despite its state of neglect, the court was quickly fixed up under the able direction of a church member, Stanley Cockerell, a South African Springbok tennis champion. He organized Sunday afternoon tennis games, which Dad encouraged as a method of bringing church members together. Besides, he liked to play tennis himself. Under Stanley Cockerell's direction, he developed a wicked serve. Non-players gathered to watch the game and enjoy afternoon tea together in the shade of the avocado tree that grew next to the tennis fence. Sometimes we had a braaivleis, or barbecue, out by the tennis court. All players arrived in their tennis whites: white shirt, white pants (usually wool flannel), or white skirt for the women, and white shoes and socks. Dad got away with wearing white shorts for the Sunday afternoon tennis match since he didn't own any long white pants.

Tennis court after renovation. View from 3rd-floor
balcony, Durban, Natal, 1950

I wasn't so lucky at defying tradition. The mother of a school
friend of mine kindly invited me to join her three children at their
tennis lessons, to make a foursome. Derryn was my best friend. We
were required to go everywhere in single file at school. Derryn and I
took turns being the shortest member of the class for many years, so
we were always at the beginning of the line together. Derryn's mother
may have thought I was deprived, being one of the youngest of such a
big family, for she had previously suggested I join Derryn at her ballet
lessons, but my parents didn't approve of ballet dancers. I believe they
must have held the opinion that ballet dancers were immoral, but they
didn't elaborate or explain. Homosexuality was not something people

talked about in front of children. The older women of the church congregation chose to advise my parents about many things, some of it wise and useful, some extremely opinionated.

At the tennis lesson, the instructor led the four of us onto the court, Derryn, her younger sister and brother, and me. He lined us up in a row, rackets in hand. As he walked along, he contorted his lips in a serious expression, looking each one of us up and down, slowly. Then he stopped and stood in front of me, whacking his racket through the air as if he were swinging at a fast-moving ball, and said, "Black tennis shoes?" in a quiet, sneering, intimidating tone of voice. Our school had recently required all girls to have a pair of black tennis shoes for gym and after-school sports. My parents couldn't afford to buy me yet another pair of shoes, a white pair, just for tennis lessons.

That was the end of my private tennis lessons.

Jeannette says she frequently played on our court with her friends. They played "round robins," which is what you do if you have a group of more than four people, each player getting a turn to play against every other player. Tennis was a required sport at our school. We used heavy wooden tennis racquets strung with animal gut that we kept in wooden presses with screws at each corner. The screws were tightened to keep the wood from losing its shape in the humid climate. Hitting a ball with a warped racquet meant you couldn't control its direction. I was very proud of the new Slazenger I was given when I grew out of my child-sized, junior Dunlop racquet. We recently retrieved those old racquets from a corner of our Florida garage so we can play with our grandchildren.

The tennis net had to be raised or lowered to regulation height before each game by turning a crank on the post at one end of the net. The net shrunk when it rained. In the days when my nose was about level with the top of the tennis net, I liked to breathe in the clean smell of the thick cotton canvas drying in the sun.

Mother grew a granadilla (passionfruit) vine on the tennis court fence. The big purple and white flowers were pretty, with delicate swirling tendrils in the middle. The sweet yellow fruit is delicious served as a topping for ice cream or mixed into cake frosting, but there is no sweet treat like a granadilla just picked from the vine, still warm from the sun, the fruit spooned out. Many people don't realize that granadilla seeds are swallowed whole. We delighted in watching unsuspecting guests from Europe or America chew the granadilla seeds. They sounded "like a rhinoceros chewing thorns," a favorite scold of Mother's when she was correcting our table manners. They saw us watching them and wondered what was wrong. Crunch, crunch. Nobody else was crunching...

The culture of a British colony is imported from "home" along with its accompanying protocols and traditions, including a certain class discrimination, sharpened by a need to hang on to whatever remains of their imagined level of distinction. There was no tolerance for "second class," whether white or black, no matter what education level had been attained. Such people were not embraced or welcomed.

Siri dressed in her tennis whites, Durban, South Africa, 1958

It was all about appearances, white shoes, not black, white skin, not black. It bred unfairness, prejudice, and snobbery. It was a tough spot for a young American girl.

WOMEN HOLD UP HALF THE SKY

THE WOMEN'S MARCH OF 1956

The 9th of August every year marks the anniversary of a seminal turning point in the history of political resistance in South Africa. On this day in 1956, South African women rose up as one to protest the planned extension of pass laws to black women.

The pass law was one of the most despised of the apartheid laws. In 1952, the government announced that black women would soon also have to carry passes. Women actively resisted this ... The now famous Women's March of 1956 was the culmination of this defiance and activism where 20,000 women marched on the Union Building in Pretoria to deliver armfuls of a petition entitled "The Demand of the Women of South Africa for the Withdrawal of Passes for Women and the Repeal of the Pass Laws," signed by women across the country, to then-Prime Minister Strijdom.

While the petition failed to halt the extension of the pass law to black women, the Women's March remains a watershed moment in South Africa, irrevocably demonstrating women's bedrock power to mobilise [sic] and fight against injustices of all kinds.

Lilian Ngoyi led the historical women's march against passes on 9 August 1956 to the Union Buildings in Pretoria. She was president of the African National Congress Women's League. Like many other apartheid activists, she was subjected to the brutal force of the apartheid government. Lilian was considered to be too dangerous... She spent most of her life either in prison in solitary confinement or banned to her house... in Mzimhlophe, Soweto, earning the dubious record of being the person who spent the longest period of time under house arrest. She died at age 69 on 13 March 1980, still under a banning order. Her name, Ngoyi, means "one who wore the plumes of the rare bird." [*South African History Archive*][28]

What Does it Mean to a Woman to Carry a Pass?

It means that homes will be broken up when women are arrested and sentenced under the pass laws; it means that helpless children will be left uncared for, when the mother is arrested and thrown into the pick-up van as she goes to buy food for her family because she has left her pass at home; it means that women and young girls will be exposed to degradation at the hands of pass-searching policemen, at the hands of 'ghost' squads with indescribable license in the dark night; it means that African women may be hired out as farm convict labour, sold for nine pence a day.

In Cape Town recently, two thousand women of all races met together under the auspices of the newly formed Cape Association to Abolish Passes for African Women—women of the Black Sash, the National Council of Women, of the Anglican Church Mother's Union, the Federation of S.A. Women, the African National Congress Women's League, the Society of Friends. Women of different races, different colours, widely differing political affiliations, came together to protest and to hear African women tell in their own words what passes meant to them. [Helen Joseph]

Helen Joseph, Secretary of the South African Federation of Women, was one of 156 persons undergoing Preparatory examination on a charge of High Treason. [Helen Joseph, *Africa South*][29]

ZEERUST

In January 1958, four people were stengunned to death at Gopane village in the Bafurutse reserve, near Zeerust. A month later all pressmen were barred from the area ... The reason for the Zeerust killings was basically that the Bantu Affairs Department had ordered the Bafurutse women to carry "passes" like their men. They were to carry them at all costs ... When the inevitable tribal disturbances followed, a 270-lb. police sergeant, Jan van Rooyen, was put in charge of operation with a squad of mobile stengun police under his command. [Dennis Kiley, *Africa South*][30]

CHAPTER 10

CHRISTMAS ANGEL: PRAYING HANDS AND CROOKED FINGERS

People have funny ideas about ministers' children. Perhaps having a father who is a minister was supposed to lend us some kind of grace? I was one of two ministers' daughters in my class at school. One of us would play Mary in the Christmas play. In the end, Frances was chosen to be Mary because, they said, she looked better than I did wearing the blue headscarf. I still remember the kind, apologetic smile Frances bestowed on me.

At the end of the school year, before we all went home for our long summer holidays, our school held an evening Carol Service. We dressed in white dresses and processed into the Hall carrying flashlights that looked like candles. Parents and siblings were invited to attend and join in singing the traditional English carols. It was one school function that my parents always attended.

When I was about ten, I was selected to be an angel in the Carol Service. A small group of us "angels" were to stand at the front of the stage in front of the choir. At the rehearsal, the teacher in charge instructed us to put the palms of our hands together as though we were praying. Part way through the rehearsal she came up on stage and spoke privately to the music teacher. Miss Munro came over and told me in a stern tone of voice to put my hands "flat, palms together," as I had been told. Mystified, I did what they told me to do. They looked at my hands. I waited, stiff with embarrassment.

"We'll have to replace her," they agreed. They wanted angelic symmetry, military uniformity. It still rings in my head. I have a crooked little finger. It won't lie flat. It used to annoy me because it collapsed whenever I tried to play a whole octave on the piano with any force. I couldn't be a Christmas angel because my little finger was crooked, something like the artist Albrecht Dürer's own finger in his drawing of *Praying Hands*? His right pinky finger doesn't look straight, either.

CHRISTMAS TRADITIONS

Christmas in our family was a mix of Swedish, German, English, and American traditions. The excitement started with the hunt for just the right Christmas tree—we were convinced that no family in Durban had a Christmas tree like ours. Most South Africans decorated Auricaria trees, similar to Norfolk pines, which we looked upon with dismay, even something like disdain—it was totally unacceptable for the trunk to show through the branches. We sometimes drove out of the city to an elderly German lady who sold "real" Christmas trees with little grey berries on them. These trees smelled like spruce trees in America. She also grew huge white climbing roses on her front porch railing which were greatly admired by Dad.

Dad would walk around the trees, his pipe tight in one corner of his mouth, exclaiming over this one and that one, until we found the tree that was the right height and evenly shaped—our tree was never stuffed into a corner of the living room because we had to be able to dance around it, so it couldn't have a good side and a not-so-good side. In addition to lights and balls we decorated the tree with strings of blue and yellow Swedish flags, a tradition inherited from our Swedish grandfather, known as CTO (for Carl Theophilus Odhner). He was also responsible for the family tradition of dancing around the tree each night before the younger ones went to bed. He had translated the Swedish Christmas song, *Juli, Julienne*, into English. Everyone, from the oldest to the youngest, joined hands and formed a circle, walking, running, or dancing around the tree as we sang. There are several verses, the dancers changing direction with each new verse:

Christmas is here, Christmas is here,
Christmas is full of joy O!
Dance around the tree, dance around the tree,
Each little girl and boy O!

The song ends with a boisterous last verse, dancers speeding up and stamping their feet: "Keep up the dance, keep up the dance, Till we can dance no longer. Then when we stop, into bed we hop, and that will make us stronger! Hooray!" with arms raised into the air and much laughter.

COOKIES AND CHRISTMAS PUDDING

When we lived in Montclair, New Jersey, where I was born, there were two families of German origin who were members of our church. They gave us their recipes for Christmas cookies: Springerle and Pfeffernüsse. Springerles are basically just flour, confectioner's sugar, and eggs. I remember being very put out when Mother decided Mike was old enough to mix the Springerles using the Mixmaster she had brought from America. It had to be connected to a transformer that gave you a shock if you touched it the wrong way. After licking the beaters and the bowl, the fun part of making Springerles has always been rolling out the dough with the special rolling pin, embossed with patterns and pictures that were transferred to the dough. The cookies were carefully cut out and placed on a cookie sheet sprinkled with anise seed—so the seeds ended up on the bottom of the cookies. The sheet of cookies was covered with a dish towel and left to "set" for about 24 hours. The next day, when the cookies were baked, the delectable smell of baking Springerles wafted throughout the house, proclaiming, "Christmas is coming!" Spicy Pfeffernüsse had bits of citron in them. Little kids usually didn't like the taste or the texture of the dried fruit. Kirstin made the Pfeffernüsse. She iced them with a clear sugar glaze.

We also made a traditional English plum pudding from a recipe supplied by our Zulu cook, Miriam. Each of us has a copy of this precious recipe, "Miriam's Christmas Pudding." We all sat around the dining table and chopped almonds, dates, and raisins into little bits. The almonds were blanched first so the skins slipped off easily, revealing the white nut underneath. Our British South African friends stirred little prizes into the dough: silver thimbles or small change, tickeys, or sixpences. They made a great ceremony of this, everyone standing around and watching. The thick, fruity dough was poured into a mold, wrapped in a cotton cloth, and steamed over a few inches of water for several hours. The puddings could be saved for weeks in colder climates, but not in the tropics. Mother served the pudding with brandy sauce, a thin custard sauce. She had to make it in two batches because some of us didn't care for the strong brandy flavor.

Rachel decorates the church for Christmas, Durban, Natal, 1957

It was my job to decorate the church for Christmas services. Piet brought me cuttings of asparagus fern that I wound around the communion rails. I collected fragrant, star-like frangipani (plumeria) flowers and poked them into the light green fern to great effect.

Church decorated for Christmas, Durban, Natal, 1952

On Christmas Day the church service began early, at nine a.m., because the sun heats up the day so quickly. Members of the congregation were invited to stay for tea after church, in our living room. This represented an interminable wait for us children. Mother was embarrassed when we made obvious glances at the tree while the lonely older church members slowly sipped their tea. With eight people in the family, there was a large pile of gifts under our tree, and we weren't allowed to open them before church.

The last ritual of the day was lighting the Christmas pudding. Dad sprinkled brandy over the dark, moist pudding as he broke it up with a big spoon. When he lit the alcohol with a match, the blue flames snapped and spread all over the pudding. As he turned the pudding with the spoon, sometimes adding more brandy to keep the flames going, Dad intoned the Latin words his father before him had recited: *Per saecula saeculorum, Odhner familia, mane in ecclesia, per saecula saeculorum,* which, translated, means, "Through ages of ages, may the Odhner family remain in the Church, through ages of ages."

From Philip and Beryl Odhner
Christmas, 1978

Beryl C. Odhner. An Atmosphere of Infants. Christmas card, 1978

In the cool of late afternoon, Dad would take us to the beach for a swim in the Indian Ocean. The Durban police were notorious for conscientiously handing out speeding tickets in the weeks surrounding Christmas. It was rumored that they used the money for their annual New Year's Eve party. So it was that one Christmas Day, with a carload of sandy kids in wet bathing suits, Dad gathered speed as he usually did so he could get up Sydenham Road without stalling. The road was especially steep at the bottom. Caught by the speed trap! The policeman came over to the driver's side window and took down Dad's details. The whole time he was talking to the policeman, Siri was hiccupping loudly in the back seat. This time Siri's tendency toward serial hiccupping served its purpose: the exasperated policeman let us go without a fine.

Durban Beach. Jeannette, Siri, Michael, and Rachel, Durban, South Africa, 1949

THE PROHIBITION OF MIXED MARRIAGES ACT, ACT No 55 of 1949

This Act made marriages between whites and members of other racial groups illegal. The police tracked down mixed couples suspected of having a relationship. Homes were invaded and doors were smashed down in the process.

Mixed couples caught in bed, were arrested ... Most couples found guilty were sent to jail. Blacks were often given harsher sentences.

It is illegal for a Marriage Officer knowingly to perform a marriage ceremony between a white and a person who is not white, and any such marriage is legally null and void. [Peter Randall, *Apartheid and the Church, Digital Innovation South Africa*][31]

THE IMMORALITY ACT, ACT NO 21 OF 1950

The Immorality Amendment Act (Act No 23 of 1957) supplemented the Prohibition of Mixed Marriages Act, made sexual intercourse, in or out of marriage, between White and Coloured or Native a punishable offence.

By 1960 it was known that more than 300 cases had been heard every year since 1951 in the magistrate's courts in all parts of the country ... Some of these cases made news; for among the accused in various provinces since 1957 were a predikant [preacher], the headmaster of a school, a well-known attorney, wealthy farmers who were married men, and the secretary to the late Prime Minister—all men whose social status was much higher than that of the men normally accused. [Julius Lewin, *Africa South*][32]

THE PROHIBITION OF MIXED MARRIAGES AMENDMENT ACT, ACT NO 21 OF 1968

If any male person who is a South African citizen or is domiciled in the Republic enters into a marriage outside the Republic which, in terms of the principal Act, cannot be solemnized within the country (because one partner is white and the other non-white), such marriage shall be void and of no effect in the Republic.

The partners to such a marriage could, thus, be prosecuted under the Immorality Act if they returned to South Africa and lived together. [Muriel Horrell, South African Institute of Race Relations, *Digital Innovation South Africa*][33]

CHAPTER 11

WILDFIRE ON THE MOUNTAIN

First family picture taken at our property, Drakensberg, Natal, 1951

When we first drove up to the Drakensberg, we stayed at the local hotel, Champagne Castle Hostel, until we could use the house my brother Pehr was building for our family vacations. Hotel guests slept in rondavels, round, thatched-roof buildings which had been built by Italian prisoners of war. We loved going to the mountains, called "the Berg" by South Africans. It took about four hours from Durban to drive to the mountains. We sat squashed together, all eight of us, one sitting forward, one leaning back. Pehr sat in front with Mother and Dad. Sometimes Siri and I sat on duffle bags stuffed with blankets and clothing, our feet out in front of us—there were no seatbelts in those days.

The Berg house, the little thatched-roof house, perched alone on the top of a hill, holds some of my deepest, most emotional memories: damp mossy woods; high craggy mountains; snakes and scorpions; and quiet nights, with their canopy of stars. The hills in front of the house seem to stretch hundreds of miles to the sea in varying shades of green and brown, with clusters of trees in the valleys. A cloud of dust rising from the dirt road just visible over the hill betrays the sense that we are completely alone in the wild. The call of an ibis, "ha-de-ha," echoing against the cliffs, captures my attention as I turn toward the mountains behind me. I follow his flight as he drifts on an air current only to float slowly down again, his moving shadow large against the cliffs in the slanting light of the afternoon sun. The mountains were sculpted long ago, of ancient basalt. With foothills sliced by deep, wooded crevasses, they catch the clouds and hold the rain until it falls in thin, crystal threads, waterfalls.

Mother once painted a picture of the Berg house. She painted each wildflower, bird, and little animal in careful detail—the lizards, an ibis, two crafty baboons hiding in the rocks, and a pair of doves. A swallow's shadow swoops against the tidy thatched roof. The little stream edged by ferns cascades down in the forefront of the picture, the water tunneling underground in places. The scene is completed by the flat-topped mountains that stand high above the serrated edges forming the backbone of the Dragon's Back. I wonder how my mother would have painted what lived in the shadow of that dragon.

Making cement blocks, Drakensberg, Natal 1952

Thatching the roof, Drakensberg, Natal, 1953

Pehr took a lot of photos to document his progress as he built the little house. The photos tell their own story, but one of the most dramatic events has no pictures. Pehr wasn't with us when we set out to climb Matterhorn. (Mike insisted that it was actually "just" a foothill of the Drakensberg, not a real mountain.) On the day we chose to climb Matterhorn, we were unaware that the forest ranger was burning a firebreak down the side of the mountain. We set off from the hostel, Dad and Kirstin, Mike, Siri, and me. We took the easier path across to Matterhorn, rather than going straight up—rain had eroded that path, creating dongas, or ditches. Firebreaks are important in protecting property from wildfire in the dry winter months, so we wouldn't have been surprised to see the smoke and flames, but this time, the wind changed direction when the men reached the bottom of the mountain, and the fire escaped their control and turned toward us.

We could hear the tension in Dad's voice as he urged us on: "Move, quickly! We have to get to a place where the grass is already burned." We couldn't turn around and go back—the flames had already blocked the way we had come, and the path led straight forward, towards the fire. Sobbing, Siri and I took great gulps of air that tasted smoky sour on our tongues. Our eyes and nostrils burned. Frantic insects landed on our faces. The freshening wind swirled little bits of burning vegetation up toward the sky. As they floated down again, wherever they landed, the dry grass caught, flames snapping, starting more fires.

Focused on getting to a safe place, we left the path and headed straight up the mountainside. Keeping our eyes on the ground in front of us, we looked for a rock or a root, anything to grab, to help ourselves up. Dad pushed us up from behind in the steep spots. When we reached an area the fire had already burned, the smoldering tufts of grass scorched our hands and jerked out of the ground, offering no traction.

We had made it up to the wide flat rocks on the top as the fire passed behind us, racing down the back of the mountain. Mike and Dad chased after the fire, hoping to somehow stop the forward movement of the flames. Kirstin stayed with Siri and me. We were dazed and frightened, trying to calm our breathing. Our big sister had a roll of spearmint candies in her pocket. She gave us each one candy at a time and instructed us to suck it, carefully, to see who could suck it the longest without breaking it. We sucked those mints till they were flat and thin.

We used up all the candies in the roll, and we forgot to cry. We had just calmed down when a huge eland walked up the hill toward us. He must have been trying to escape the fire too. We didn't move. The large antelope can be more than six feet high at the shoulder and weigh up to 1200 lbs. We were not unaware of his size, or that he was topped with long, spiral horns. Thankfully, the eland didn't choose to share the stony mountaintop with us. He stared at us for a few moments, haughtily flicking his tail, then turned and walked away.

Property viewed from Matterhorn (note firebreaks), Drakensberg, Natal, 1958. Annotated by Michael Odhner, 2015

At last, hot and exhausted, Dad and Mike came back to where we waited. They decided to take the quickest way home, straight down the mountainside, sliding on our backsides. We grabbed burnt tufts of grass, put our feet on rocks, trying to slow our forward momentum. Hot and thirsty, with streaks of black soot on our faces and hands, we must have been a frightful sight to greet our Mother, who had stayed behind at the house, completely unaware of our encounter with the fire.

There weren't many hikes that were suitable for small children in the Drakensberg. The only paths that were kept in good shape on any regular basis were the "contour" paths, maintained by the forest rangers. If you could climb that far, the paths were wider, flatter, and cleared of any obstructions or washed-out areas. But it took time to get up there.

Destructive wildfires burn for miles in the winter dry season, so it is critically important to prepare firebreaks to protect your house and land. The forest rangers control the bigger burns in the mountains, while the farmers and property owners burn their own firebreaks to protect homes and fields. When a fire escapes, whole hillsides and miles of veld burn black. Armies of orange flames line up in the night where wild fires are still burning after dark.

The best time to burn a break is early morning, before the wind rises. On the day of our hike up Matterhorn the ranger's "boys" were nearly finished burning from the top to the base of the mountain. It was the change in wind direction that endangered us, and as nobody official knew we were there, they must have been as surprised and horrified as we were, if they noticed us at all. Pehr hired local Zulu men to help burn our firebreaks. We would have called them "native boys." Armed with wattle branches, some of us joined in and beat the flames on the near edge of the fire so it would burn in the other direction. There was always a lot of shouting and gesticulating and running after flames that tried to escape.

When my sister Kirstin was in college, she conducted an experiment: she buried a special thermometer in the ground where the fire was going to burn. Her professor wanted her to test the temperature of the soil below the surface at a measured number of inches. Unfortunately, and perhaps not unexpectedly, the thermometer broke. Kirstin also collected botanical specimens. She and some of her college friends once made a special journey into the mountains to find plants to preserve in their wooden plant presses.

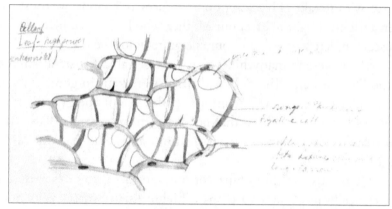

Kirstin Odhner. Botanical drawing, University of Natal, Pietermaritzburg, 1955

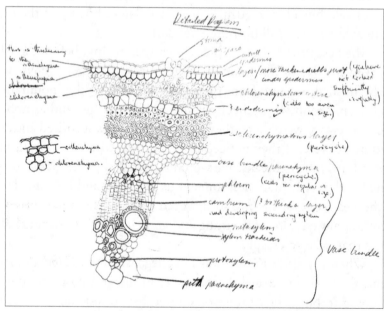

Kirstin Odhner. Botanical drawing, University of Natal, Pietermaritzburg, 1955

Among all the memories I have of living in South Africa, our trips to the Berg are the most precious. We loved that little house, facing the mountains in one direction and looking out toward the flowing, grassy veld in the other. In summer we could watch the progress of crashing thunderstorms from miles away, and on quiet, cloudless nights in winter we'd feel blessed under the bright sea of stars. We learned to share the wilderness with the birds and snakes, the baboons and scorpions, and yes, maybe even a hyena or a leopard passing by. Its vast remote beauty still holds first place in our hearts.

The Berg House, Drakensberg, Natal, 1953

THE SUPPRESSION OF COMMUNISM ACT, Act No. 44 of 1950

The Act sanctioned the banning/punishment of any group or individual intending to bring about "any political, industrial, social or economic change in the Union by the promotion of disturbances or disorder, by unlawful acts or omissions or by the threat of such acts and omissions." The definition of Communism was so broad and crude that its liberal opponents suspected it was seeking also to trap liberals in its net. Renamed the **Internal Security Act** in 1976. [*South African History Online*][34]

SOUTH AFRICA IN CRISIS

All through these years opponents of the Government have been silenced. With the skillful use of propaganda, the bogey of Communism has been magnified, and the **Suppression of Communism Act** has been used to ban, put under house arrest, detain or charge anyone who has the temerity to oppose them publicly, and to charge them with furthering the aims of Communism. Political organizations have been declared unlawful and for the non-Whites, certainly, all avenues of legitimate protest have been closed. The S.A.B.C. pours out incessant propaganda on Communism and equates it with liberalism and, in fact, with all criticism of Government policy. [Jean Sinclair, *The Black Sash*][35]

"As minister of Posts and Telegraphs, I want to say to those people who send reports overseas slandering South Africa that they must not expect of me that all their reports will reach their destination." [Franz Erasmus, *Africa South*][36]

The Nationalist government blamed hostile journalists for their image in the world. The journalists were viewed as "agents or dupes of Moscow." Helen Suzman once summed it up perfectly in parliament when a cabinet minister, goaded by her perpetual questions about abuses of civil rights, yelled at her,

"You put these questions just to embarrass South Africa overseas."

To which she replied, *"It is not my questions that embarrass South Africa—it is your answers."*
[Benjamin Pogrund, *The War of Words*][37]

THE RIOTOUS ASSEMBLIES AND SUPPRESSION OF COMMUNISM ACT, ACT NO 15 OF 1954

Outlawed Communism and the Communist Party in South Africa. Communism was defined so broadly that it covered any call for radical change. "Communists" could be banned from participating in a political organization and restricted to a particular area. The Act empowered the Minister of Justice "to prohibit listed persons from being members of specific organisations or from attending gatherings of any description without giving them the opportunity of making representations in their defence or furnishing reasons."

The act also allowed the Minister to ban publications deemed to incite hostility between groups and thus could be used to ban publications which tried to bring about social change.[38]

Repealed by the **Internal Security Act, Act No 74** of 1982.

BANNING
Mrs. Sonia Bunting, who is under 24-hour house arrest, has been refused permission by the Chief Magistrate of Cape Town to resume her job as Cape Town finance collector for *New Age*. She has also been refused permission to take her daughter Margaret for oboe lessons once a week in Oranjezicht. The Chief Magistrate gave Mrs. Bunting permission to visit a medical specialist for attention provided

that she advised the office in charge of the Security Police prior to the visit and returned home immediately after the conclusion of the consultation. [*New Age*][39]

[Sonia Bunting was the wife of Brian Bunting, editor of *New Age* and author of the book, *Rise of the South African Reich*.]

CHAPTER 12

THE WATTLE WOODS

*Feodor Pitcairn. Old stone bridge over the Pennypack
Creek, Bryn Athyn, Pennsylvania, 2012*

Woods and forests are a recurring theme in our family's history. Where we lived in Pennsylvania, the Pennypack Creek flows through miles and miles of beautiful woodland as it winds its way to the Delaware River. A walk in the woods has been a favorite recreation for generations. The younger children always look forward to playing "Pooh sticks" on the old stone bridge over the creek, which was named "Pennicpacka" by the Leni-Lenape, the Native Americans who once lived in the area.

Beryl Odhner. Family group, Lake Wallenpaupack, 1946

Dad built the family's first vacation home on the shores of Lake Wallenpaupack in the forest-clad Pocono Mountains. The lake was created in 1926 when the Pennsylvania Power and Light Company built a dam across the Wallenpaupack River. The original inhabitants of this far northeast corner of Pennsylvania were the Leni-Lenape, who hunted bear in the woods and fished in the river. Dad took the older kids fishing and taught them how to swim and paddle a canoe. Mother painted colorful designs on the wooden walls inside the house. So our family's love of woods and trees was born by the Pennypack and encouraged by excursions into the lakeside forests of the Pocono Mountains. On the other side of the Atlantic, we explored indigenous yellow-wood forests in the deep ravines of the Little Berg and played in the wattle woods skirting our property.

The house on Lake Wallenpaupack was sold when the family moved to South Africa in 1948. The proceeds were used to help purchase property in the Drakensberg, where Pehr built the thatched, cinderblock house during his college vacations. After sitting squeezed together in the car for hours, we knew we were finally getting there when Dad turned onto a side road—really just two strips of earth with a hump of grass in the middle. The driveway took us through the wattle woods and up over the hill to the house.

My little sister Siri and I liked to play in the wattle woods at the edge of our property. It was a magical place. The early morning dew left buds of water on the delicate webs that decorated the bright green moss, like the shiny silver beads of mercury that run all over when you break an old-fashioned thermometer. The damp air felt fresh and cool on our bare arms. It was quiet in the woods, except for the sound of moisture dripping from the leaves. I whispered to Siri, "Maybe a fairy came in the night?"

Rachel and Siri hanging laundry (note wattle woods in background and barbed wire fencing), Drakensberg, Natal, 1956

Siri and I had come to check on the fairy houses we'd made the day before. The cool, shadowy darkness was such a contrast to the warm, bright sun outside the woods that it was like stepping into a big dark room in another world. I don't think either of us really and truly believed in fairies, but it was fun to pretend. British South African children grew up with fantasy tales of elves and fairies, goblins, gnomes, Scottish pixies, and Irish leprechauns. Some of the books I remember were beautifully illustrated, like *Flower Fairies of the Spring*, by Cicely Mary Barker [Blackie, 1923]. Superstition and magic were part of the Zulu culture, too, so our belief in invisible little people mingled with local folklore. Miriam, our cook, told us about the Tokoloshe, an evil water sprite that climbs up out of the water to grab you. And, too, in church we were taught about angels, how they are present with us even though we can't see them.

Beryl C. Odhner. Fairies in the Woods. Detail from unpublished manuscript, The Clothespin Dolls Who Ran Away, ca 1975

The wattle woods was over the hill, out of view from the house. We were small girls and they didn't want us to wander about alone. There were snakes and scorpions and other dangers in that wilderness—like big black Friesland cows—so we were glad that our brother Michael accompanied us. There were no paths through the woods, but we easily found our favorite mossy spot. Mike poked about, looking for branches to make walking sticks. We liked to have new ones each year as we had usually grown a few inches. Walking sticks are essential to life at the Berg: you must sweep and swat at the grass in front of you as you walk along to scare away snakes.

Mike's penknife was precious to him, as its ownership elevated him to the realm of grownup men. He used the knife to strip off rough bits of bark and little branches, feeling the smooth wet surface with his finger. The little noises he made were comforting, made us feel safe, less alone, but they alarmed the birds that were gathered in the tree-tops. They flapped away, calling out their raucous song, "Piet-my-vrou, Piet-my-vrou," in chorus (Afrikaans for 'Pieter my wife'). If you pay close attention, you will hear the plaintive three-note cry of this little bird (the Red-chested Cuckoo) in the background of movies filmed in Africa. Pehr preferred the Zulu name, *Uphezukomkhono*, which means something like "hoe on the arm" or, "time to get to work." He could pronounce it perfectly, with all the right click sounds.

Beryl C. Odhner. Little Herd Boys. Detail from color pencil drawing, from unpublished manuscript, Jabula, ca 1938

Sometimes the herd of big black cows wandered through the woods. The sharp sounds of twigs snapping warned us well before they came too near. Perhaps they were looking for shade, or maybe the woods were on the way to wherever they spent the day. Little Zulu boys of six or seven years old herded the family cattle, but I was not convinced of their ability to control the big animals even though they are quite amenable to being sent on their way by a small boy armed with nothing but a short stick and an ability to whistle.

I was afraid of cows—when they were all bunched together, you couldn't tell which one might be the bull. My father's grandfather had died when he was gored by a bull, long ago in Sweden, so Dad was afraid of them, too, but wouldn't usually admit it. They erected a barbed wire fence around the berg house, saying it was because "Rachel is afraid of the cows." After that, we were safely on our side of the fence when the herd of cattle streamed past morning and evening.

Mr, Jameson with Daisy the cow, Drakensberg, Natal, 1954

But we were not afraid of Mr. Jameson's cow, Daisy. She was a beautiful light brown Jersey cow. Mr. Jameson showed us how to milk her. We giggled when she licked our arms with her long, sandpapery tongue. We got delicious, creamy milk from Daisy, who was kept in a fenced-in field behind our house.

Mr. Jameson was a good neighbor: he gave Pehr valuable advice on hiring local labor and helped him obtain building supplies. He instructed him on how to install a pump in our stream that would send water up the hill to fill the big, round corrugated iron water tank next to the house. Pehr needed the water early on to make the concrete blocks he used to build the walls. The Jamesons' house was cozy, comfortable and dark, decorated with animal skins on the walls and floors, very different from our airy, light cottage with views from all the windows. Our furniture was utilitarian, the only soft seating being the studio couch where Pehr slept. Mom and Dad had a real bed, but the rest of us slept on military issue folding canvas camp cots. We made the cots up with old prickly woolen blankets in the winter, some with moth holes in them.

When our family stayed at the berg house, Mother cooked our meals on a kerosene stove, and we used an Aladdin oil lamp to light the house after dark. Dad read to us by the softly glowing lamplight after supper. One of our favorite books was *Little House in the Big Woods*, by Laura Ingalls Wilder. The stories of Laura and Mary in the woods of Wisconsin fed our imagination about what life in America must be like.

After we returned from South Africa, my sister Kirstin and her husband bought a vacation cottage at Lake Wallenpaupack. Our parents also had a place at the lake, so all the grandchildren had the opportunity to play in the woods. "Arrowheading" was a favorite pastime. Kirstin had a collection of flint Indian arrowheads she found in the shallow water along the edges of the lake. Other members of the family who found flint arrowheads were gently persuaded to add them to Kirstin's collection, which she mounted and cataloged. She eventually gave her collection to the Smithsonian.

Mother was ingenious at coming up with things for children to do when they weren't swimming in the lake or if the weather was cold.

One year she made and dressed clothespin dolls for the little girls to play with, and wrote and illustrated a story about two clothespin dolls who ran away and were lost in the woods. It was handwritten, with watercolor illustrations. After she passed away, we found a treasure trove of her art that she hadn't shared with the family. It included a typed version of her Clothespin Dolls story with pen and ink illustrations. The magic of the woods must have been more important to her than we knew. She wanted to make sure her love of the woods was passed on to younger generations.

*   *   *

When I eventually returned to the Berg, thirty years later, I didn't recognize the driveway to the cottage—where was the wattle woods, I worried? An empty feeling took hold of me. We walked on up the road to the house, which didn't look right, either. When we introduced ourselves to the new owners of the property, they were friendly, pleased to meet us, and told us there were "good vibes" in that house and they could feel it was a happy home. They explained that a lumber company had planted Daisy's field with pine trees. In a terrible lightning storm, the pine trees had caught fire, the flames spreading to the thatch roof, and the house was destroyed. Dad had always feared lightning at the berg because of that thatched roof.

The new owners had rebuilt the house using Pehr's architectural plans, except, and here they smiled, they had added a kitchen, and an indoor bathroom replaced the old outhouse. They said all the wattle trees in the woods had been cut down by local African farmers for use as fuel. Sixty years later, and in spite of the new Mandela government and an expanded rural electrification program, it was still difficult to serve all the widespread pockets of population with electricity. Kerosene and lamp oil were beyond the reach of poor, rural farmers, and the wattle wood was free, except for the labor of cutting it.

I was so disappointed. I had longed to experience the magic of that childhood place again, to smell the damp forest floor, and touch the soft blanket of moss where fantasy and reality joined to create sweet memories.

The woods in the Pennypack watershed are now protected by the Pennypack Ecological Trust and other conservation organizations. Northern Pennsylvania's vast woodlands are preserved as State Forests. The Drakensberg area is a UNESCO World Heritage site. But what of the wattle woods that was nestled over the hill near the little house we loved so much? Like the smoke from the wildfire that chased us up the mountain so many, many years ago, the wattle woods are gone.

———⟶✹⟵———

THE BANTU AUTHORITIES ACT, ACT NO 68 OF 1951

Established Bantu tribal, regional, and territorial authorities in the regions set out for Africans under the Group Areas Act, and it abolished the Natives Representative Council. The Bantu authorities were to be dominated by chiefs and headmen appointed by the government. The Act provided for the establishment of black homelands.
This Act was introduced to reinforce the South African government's policy of "separate development" of the races. Two decades later, in 1970, **The Bantu Homelands Citizenship Act** made every African a citizen of one of the tribal homelands, no matter where they lived, which effectively excluded them from holding South African citizenship.

The Bantu homelands were established in areas with infertile soil, and in some cases the homelands were divided into separate, non-contiguous areas.

Report on a Trip to Rural areas of the Transvaal
I also learned from doctors and nurses in the mission hospitals what a medical emergency meant: if a woman in a distant kraal, a collection of huts inside a fence, experi-

enced difficulties during labor, they said, she was put on a sled, which was dragged across country to the nearest track while someone set off with a message for the hospital to send an ambulance to an agreed meeting place.

By the time the woman and the ambulance met up, which could be three or more days later, it was likely that the baby was dead. By the time the ambulance reached the hospital, the mother could be dead. I also learned that no one had any real idea about the size of the black population: few births were registered and few deaths. The five-yearly census was at best a rough guess about numbers. [Benjamin Pogrund, *War of Words*][40]

CHAPTER 13

ZULU KRAAL

I had often wondered what it would be like to live in a grass hut. I once wrote an imaginary story about a little Zulu girl for a school writing assignment. I named her Tembe—she lived in a grass hut in a kraal. I had asked our cook, Miriam, what would be a good name for my fictional little girl.

Digging a well with Mr. Jameson (note Zulu kraal in background), 1954

There was a kraal, a group of huts, just over the hill from our berg house. We could hear sounds at night after dark when the quiet had descended all around: a dog barking, a child's high voice, men calling out to each other; and sometimes we heard them singing in their melodious language.

Once we were invited to visit a kraal. They greeted us shyly. The women and children were barefoot, their feet pressing into the soft sandy earth. Inside the hut there was a wonderful smell of warm sundried grass, smoky from a wood fire. There were clay storage pots and grass mats. The floor of hard-packed earth was swept clean, sprinkled with water to keep down the dust. A thin yellow mongrel dog sniffed around us and slunk away, chasing the chickens that pecked in the ground, hoping to find a kernel of maize.

Zulu woman and children, Drakensberg, Natal, 1953

I longed to experience life in the kraal, a place that seemed to me to be free of the many restrictions in my life. There was a feeling of being at one with the earth and the mountain air, the fragrant veld grass laying a bouquet over everything.

THE NATIVES RESETTLEMENT ACT, ACT NO 19 OF 1954

The Act empowered the Government to remove Africans from any area within and next to the magisterial district of Johannesburg and their settlement elsewhere.

SOPHIATOWN

Life in Sophiatown. Sophiatown developed its own colourful character and history. The houses were built according to people's ability to pay, their own tastes, and cultural background. As a result, there were some houses that were built of brick, and may have had four or more rooms; some were much smaller. Others were built like people's homes in the rural areas; while still others may have been single room shacks put together with corrugated iron and scrap sheet metal. Perhaps more importantly, Sophiatown developed a sense of community like no other. People struggled to survive together, and a rich culture based on shebeens, mbaqanga music, and beer-brewing developed. People remember Sophiatown fondly.

The Destruction of Sophiatown. Two days before the removals were scheduled to take place, 2000 police, armed with automatic rifles, invaded Sophiatown and started moving out the first families... . That first night, in the pouring rain, 110 families were moved out of Sophiatown to the new township of Meadowlands in Soweto. The removal of all the families, and the physical destruction of Sophiatown took several years. [*South African History Online*][41]

THE STRATEGIES OF BANTU RESETTLEMENT

In Natal we are confronted with two main aspects of Bantu resettlement: those of the rural areas and those of urban areas. In addition, … Natal is faced with the task of resettling the population of **Black Spots**. Some 200 of these areas remain to be cleared. The conditions under which the inhabitants of most of them live are an indictment of any nation which claims to number itself among the advanced states of the world. Many are, indeed, Black Spots in more ways than one, sited on ruined, donga-scarred soil, with disease-ridden slum housing. Where there is water, it is usually polluted.

As a result of land betterment schemes, **scattered kraals** will have to be relocated at a more rapid rate and their occupants resettled in village-type groups. [Lawrence Morgan, *Black Sash News*][42]

BLACK SPOTS

Recently the Minister of Bantu Administration and Development announced that he was about to set out on a programme which would finally get rid of "black spots" in white areas. There are several hundred "black spots" in South Africa, but what precisely are they and why do they offend the Minister?

A black spot is an area in which Africans own land in freehold. Their title is on paper no different from that of the white people who are their neighbours. In most cases the freehold rights have been held and highly cherished by the African people concerned for several generations. Black spots are of several kinds: in some cases they are farms owned by individuals. Some are farms bought by tribal communities at the beginning of the century. Some are areas bought by a group of individuals who combined their limited resources to buy land which they later subdivided into residential plots. Some are suburbs of residential townships. Often these last have been encroached upon by later expansion of the "white" part of the town. But whatever its origins, the land in every black spot was *legally* bought by African people. [*Liberal Opinion*][43]

REMOVALS

About 200 African tenants were made homeless after tractors towing a steel cable demolished 21 huts on a farm belonging to P. H. van der Westhuizen in November last year. The farmer had got a court order in Weenen Magistrate's Court to evict the Africans as illegal 'squatters.' ... By May, 1972, it was reported that scores of farm workers and their children were starving in the Msinga Reserve. The *Natal Mercury* reporter wrote that pellagra, malnutrition sores, incipient kwashiorkor, and loss of weight were clearly evident.

The older residents already living in real poverty objected to their presence. The newcomers had no firewood and the other residents objected to their using cow dung as a substitute because they had no stock. The farm workers dumped in the area have to live under canvas or crude wattle and daub. On rainy days, their clothes and furniture are soaked, and the bags of mealies brought from Weenen also become saturated. [David Hemson, *Reality*][44]

Chapter 14

The Quality of Night

The quality of night is different in the mountains. It is tangible. In the evening, when the sun's rays slide up off the veld, their cold fingers paint the mountainside in pale color, like a faded canvas. Draped in shadows, the mountains lose their distinctive shapes.

It's wintertime at the Drakensberg. After supper, the family is sitting quietly, tired from a day outdoors. The big black kettle on the potbellied stove hisses: it must be almost empty. Mother is hooking a rag rug—she needs to keep her hands busy. Perhaps she's thinking of putting it on the cold floor in the next room, next to her side of the old double bed. Mike whittles a stick with his penknife, collecting the shavings together so as not to make a mess. He is concentrating on smoothing the wood. The walking sticks he'd made for us stand in the corner by the back door.

Pehr sits with his legs stretched out, his arms across his chest—he's wearing the green wool pullover Mother knitted for him. His face is sunburned, his eyes are closed. In the dim light, Kirstin checks her notes on an experiment for botany class, her cigarette sending up a thin curl of smoke. We made ashtrays from the clay Mike dug out of the little stream down the hill. We dried the ashtrays in the hot sun, their wavy edges exhibit the pinches from our little fingers. Jeannette, her hair in untidy braids, plays solitaire—the cards slap, snapping out of her hand onto the oilcloth table covering.

Siri and I are huddled together on the bench at the end of the table, our legs swinging slowly, eyelids drooping, watching the shadows thrown onto the walls by the soft glow of the oil lamp. Siri's well-worn brown sweater is missing some buttons. She must be cold. Since we live in the tropics, we don't have a lot of warm clothes, so when warmth from the potbellied stove can no longer compete with cold air seeping through the cracks around the windows, and the cement floor turns cold under our feet, the best way to get warm is to get into bed.

Dad had played a hand of cards with us and read one of the stories about Kalulu the hare from the book, *The Long Grass Whispers*[45] by Geraldine Elliot. When he knocks the tobacco out of his pipe on the edge of his ashtray—the sharp sound magnified by the very depth of the quiet—that's the signal for us to go outside and brush our teeth. Slowly, muttering complaints, Siri and I follow him outside to the water tank. The flame from the lantern he carries serves only to make the banished shadows dance as if they are laughing at us. We brush and spit into the muddy puddle under the tap. The crunch of our feet on the brittle, dry ground is loud, startling, in the cold night air, so crisp we can almost taste it. It's important to whisper in the presence of the myriad of stars overhead. Dad likes to quote from Genesis, where the Lord says to Abraham, "Now look toward the heavens, and count the stars, if you are able to count them" [Gen.15:5].

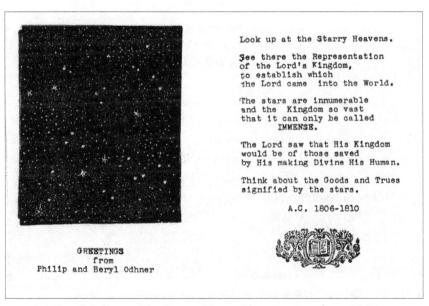

Look up at the Starry Heavens.

See there the Representation
of the Lord's Kingdom,
to establish which
the Lord came into the World.

The stars are innumerable
and the Kingdom so vast
that it can only be called
    IMMENSE.

The Lord saw that His Kingdom
would be of those saved
by His making Divine His Human.

Think about the Goods and Trues
signified by the stars.

        A.C. 1806-1810

GREETINGS
from
Philip and Beryl Odhner

Beryl Odhner. The Starry Skies. Christmas card, ca 1965

Shivering, we hurry back inside. We haven't yet learned to be still and appreciate the quality of night in that vast wilderness.

It's comforting to go to bed with the rest of the family just a few feet away on the other side of our makeshift wall of flattened cardboard boxes. In place of a door, an old Navajo weaving hangs from a heavy beam across the open space, a colorful reminder of another place.

The night sounds are different in the mountains. Lying in our camp cots under thin old woolen blankets, scarred with moth holes, we listen to the end-of-the-day sounds: Mother filling a pot with water for the next morning's oatmeal; Pehr opening the door to look outside, wondering what the next day's weather will be like. He has disturbed a lizard that rustles about in the thick thatch grass over our heads.

We can just hear the Zulus singing in the kraal over the hill: their voices rising and falling like waves in a lilting lullaby.

But it is our Dad who gives the final embrace to the end of the day. Like a benediction, he sings, softly, lovingly, in his beautiful deep voice:

"Swing low, sweet chariot .... comin' for to carry me home."

NATIVE URBAN AREAS AMENDMENT ACT, ACT NO 69 OF 1956

This Act enables an urban local authority to order an African to leave its area if it is considered that his presence is detrimental to the maintenance of peace and order. Should this be done, the local authority, if so requested, will move the African's dependents and personal effects to his new place of residence, charging any costs to the municipal Native Revenue Account. [Muriel Horrell, *Digital Innovation South Africa*][46]

[The Act] was enacted to remove such concentrations of Blacks such as servants living in central city blocks of flats. Verwoerd suggested that *"the arbitrary number of five Black servants per block of flats was a 'wise' number to prevent overcrowding."* [*O'Malley Archives, Nelson Mandela Foundation*]⁴⁷

Zanyokwe—For Betterment or Worse?

Resettlement, in Government terms, aims at clearing "non-productive Bantu" or "redundant blacks" from white areas, and sending them to resettlement camps or back to their homelands.

"Non-productive Bantu" have been classified by the Government as: the aged, unfit widows, women with dependent children, families who do not qualify for Section 10 rights, superfluous farm labourers and squatters.

Ironically, even professional blacks, such as doctors, attorneys, agents, traders and industrialists have fallen into this category because they do not fit into the so-called "white" economy. [Marian Lacy, *The Black Sash*]⁴⁸

CHAPTER 15

A QUICK TRIP TO AMERICA

U.S. Consular Service. Passport photo, Durban, South Africa, 1956

We were going to America—on a ship! Michael, Siri, and I poured over the colorful, glossy brochures Dad brought home from the travel agent, captivated by the diagrams of the ship's decks with the cabins mapped out, showing tiny beds, chairs, sinks, and portholes. We chose the rooms we wanted, and then changed our minds and chose rooms on other decks.

African ministers came to the docks to wish
us Bon Voyage, Durban, 1956

In 1956 the whole family was required to go back to America to renew our U.S. citizenship. We sailed on an American steamship, the *African Endeavor*. It was small, compared to modern cruise ships, with only one hundred and fifty passengers. We had an intensely enjoyable adventure—three weeks crossing the Atlantic from the southern tip of Africa to New York City. Friends came down to the Durban docks to wish us *Bon Voyage*. Even some of the African ministers came.

On board ship we ate American food: thick "griddle cakes" for breakfast, with plenty of real maple syrup, and there was a whole glass of orange juice for each of us. The pancakes mother made were thin, and our syrup was melted sugar with, sometimes, a dash of artificial maple flavor stirred in. None of us liked the thick Lyle's Golden Syrup that South Africans use. I don't mean to imply that we didn't enjoy Mother's pancakes: griddle cakes were just so thick and satisfying. At home we each had the juice of one hand-squeezed orange at breakfast, measuring less than an inch in the glass, the taste spoiled by the cod liver oil mother made us swallow before we drank the juice.

For a few months before we flew to South Africa in 1948, we had stayed at Caprice, an old farmhouse in Bryn Athyn surrounded by maple trees. Pehr, who was fourteen years old at the time, tapped the trees, collecting the sap in little buckets. He boiled it down until he had made maple syrup. It takes a lot of sap to produce just a little bit of syrup, so it was carefully doled out. On the ship, there was a whole jug full of maple syrup on each table, with refills if we wanted more. The syrup was served in clever little jugs with handles that opened the spout so you could pour the syrup out neatly. We ate a lot of pancakes on that voyage.

In the afternoons, iced tea in tall glasses was served on deck by smartly uniformed waiters, called stewards. We had never heard of drinking cold tea, with ice. Only hot tea is served in British colonial countries, even after a vigorous tennis game on a warm day—they claimed it cooled you by opening up the pores.

One of the crewmen on the African Endeavor, whose name was "Tex" (he was a Texan), had, coincidentally, served on the same ship my father sailed on when he was seventeen. Dad and some friends "ran away" to sea after graduating from high school. One of thirteen children (he was number eleven), orphaned by the age of ten, he and his younger brothers were passed around between their older married siblings until old enough to move into the dormitory at the high school at the Academy of the New Church in Bryn Athyn. His sister Ione lived in Durban with her husband, a New Church minister, Rev. Elmo Acton. Dad stayed with them the time he visited South Africa as a young man.

The owner of the shipping line, Mr. Farrell—of the same company that later owned the *African Endeavor*—accepted the young men on board to keep company with his own son, who also happened to be aboard that trip. He didn't want the boys to mix with the rough crewmen, so they were all placed under the care of the captain. To earn their passage, they did their share of hard work, like scrubbing decks and painting.

Our large cabin on the *African Endeavor* was at the end of the corridor, near the stern of the ship. Dad made an arrangement with Tex that he would climb through a porthole into our cabin, even though this was strictly forbidden. Crew members were not allowed to mix with passengers, for the safety of the passengers, I assume. Seamen could be rough-mannered and crude. Tex and Dad had fun talking about their earlier shared experiences.

Tex returned a second time and brought with him a children's illustrated copy of Longfellow's *Song of Hiawatha*, which he presented to me, perhaps because I reminded him of somebody, or maybe because I was just the right age to enjoy it. I've always treasured that book, and so have my children. It was filled with colorful pictures of tall Indian warriors; old men making flint arrowheads; girls in deerskin and moccasins decorated with little colored beads; Old Nokomis; a papoose; and the little squirrel, Adjidomo (tail-in-the-air), who became a favorite of my older son. The world of Hiawatha, filled with pictures of the life and mythology of woodland Indians, was a different world from Africa. I loved the poem, "On the shores of Gitche Gumee."

Leaving Durban, the ship sailed south down the coast to East London, Port Elizabeth, and Cape Town. As we neared the Cape, the ship rolled and pitched in the high, rough waves known as the "Cape rollers." The captain explained that the turbulence is created by ocean currents where the Atlantic and the Indian Oceans meet—where the warm-water Agulhas current, moving down the east coast of South Africa, meets the cold water of the west coast Benguela current, and turns back on itself. Stewards attached little railings to the edges of the dining tables to prevent the dishes from slipping off and smashing to the floor.

Not everybody visited the dining room when the sea was rough. The rocking motion of the ship made my older sisters seasick. Kirstin and Jeannette lay in bed moaning and said they couldn't eat anything. They refused to go up on deck, even though standing on deck in the fresh air and looking at the horizon is said to be the best cure for seasickness as it reconnects the brain and the eye to the inner ear. But I had caught Dad's infectious love of the sea. I loved the rocking movement of the ship and fell asleep in my top bunk listening to the comforting creaking sounds as the ship rolled over and back again (yes, steel ships do creak). Only once in a while did I wonder what would happen if it stayed over on its side and didn't roll back up again.

In Cape Town we rode a cable car to the top of Table Mountain and gazed way down on what looked like the end of the world. The southernmost tip of the African continent is actually Cape Agulhas, southeast of the Cape peninsula. After leaving Cape Town, the ship made a stop at the island of Saint Helena, where Napoleon had lived in exile. Days after leaving land behind, coming upon a mountainous island in the middle of the sea is startling. I saw only a grey-green wall. "That's Saint Helena. There it is, right in front of you." I just couldn't take it in—the sea was flat the day before. I thought an island would be a little bump in the ocean that would grow bigger as we sailed closer, over a period of hours. That had happened overnight, of course. Gradually, as various physical features began to stand out, like valleys and little buildings, it became clearer to me that it was land.

We were expected to leap up onto the concrete wharf from the pitching rowboat that took us into the port. Enthusiastic, brown-skinned men shouted at us to reach up and grab their hands so they could pull us ashore. It looked risky. The side of the wharf was slippery with barnacles, and the water between the pitching rowboat and the wharf was black and very deep, but we did it, with lots of cheerful, noisy encouragement from the locals.

The first place we visited was Napoleon's house. I wondered what it would be like to be exiled, to never be permitted to visit your home country again. Perhaps Mother and Dad felt somewhat exiled in South Africa? Napoleon's house, preserved as a museum, is set high on a hilltop, with a beautiful view and a flower garden. I've read that it wasn't in such good repair when Napoleon lived there, and he must have been lonely.

He had a big, wooden bathtub. It would have used a lot of hot water to fill that tub. I remembered Napoleon's wooden bathtub years later when looking at the painting of Citizen Marat, who was stabbed by the royalist Charlotte Corday. In that painting, *Death of Marat,* by Jacques-Louis David, the victim is sitting in a wooden bathtub, shaped like a wooden shoe, a *sabot.* Perhaps that is the rather dubious connection in my mind. But where else have you seen a wooden bathtub?

From Saint Helena, we sailed northwest across the equator, where we were treated to a visit from King Neptune, god of the sea. Crossing the equator is traditionally a rite of passage, a time for mock trials on board ship. Women passengers were blindfolded and guided to put their hands in a rotten tomato, supposed to represent Admiral Lord Nelson's blinded eye, though I have no idea what he had to do with Neptune. The men were made to walk the plank—landing in the ship's swimming pool. My beautiful sister Jeannette, eighteen years old, was chosen to be Neptune's queen. She sat next to Neptune on a makeshift throne, her lovely red hair decorated with sea weed.

There was one thing we had to do on that trip that we did not like at all: Mike, Siri, and I were expected to do schoolwork every morning, to keep up with our South African classes, especially Latin and mathematics. Dad was in charge of teaching me math. In an effort to improve my grades, I had been sent to a tutor who touched me inappropriately. After I cried and refused to go back to the next tutoring session, Mother asked my gentle sister, Jeannette, if she could find out what was wrong. I didn't return to the math tutor, even though he had been highly recommended. Then the math teacher at my school, Miss Keane, ordered me to stand up in front of the class one day. She proceeded to harangue me, "Why aren't you good at math like your sisters?" Dad was not patient with me, either, so my kind brother Michael took over this task on the ship. Thankfully, the classes ended when Mother and Dad realized that nobody was paying attention. There were just too many distractions. And, after all, we would be attending school in America, even if for only a few months.

Dad shared with us his interest in everything that had to do with the ship and the sea. He introduced us to silvery flying fish—some even landed on the deck of the ship—and the Sargasso Sea, a mat of floating seaweed that spread for miles in all directions, serving as an incubator for all sorts of sea life. Together we delighted in the mysterious bioluminescent organisms that glow in the dark under the surface of the water. Dad called them "phosphorescence." Every afternoon at four o'clock the captain posted the ship's position, using little colored pins on a big map outside the bridge. Dad took us to see how far we'd come and how close we were to New York, the end of our journey. He was excited. He was going home.

We entered New York harbor on a foggy February morning, greeted by a cold wind iced with sleet. Huddled close at the ship's rail, colder than I can ever remember feeling, I looked where Dad was pointing, again telling me to "Look there, straight ahead." I couldn't see anything through the swirling white mist. I could feel the vibration of the foghorn shuddering through my feet, and I wondered why he had woken us up at six in the morning and dragged us up onto the deck. Wait ... there she was ... the Statue of Liberty! She was so beautiful, so welcoming, holding up that torch to light our way into the heart of America. Tears filled my eyes. I was just one of so many thousands of others who must have felt the same overwhelming emotion, but for the first time in my life, I felt I could truly feel that I was an American.

*Photographer unknown. Philip Odhner, third
from left, Atlantic Ocean, ca 1925*

Members of our family—and our ancestors—have crossed the Atlantic Ocean many times. Our mother's ancestors, fleeing religious or political persecution, sailed from England, Scotland, Wales, and Ireland, some of them making the crossing as early as the mid-seventeenth century in wooden sailing ships. Our father's father came from Sweden and entered the U.S. through Ellis Island in the mid-eighteenth century. His mother's origins were English, French, and Greek, her forebears from England arriving at the time of William Penn.

My own father sailed to South Africa as a boy of seventeen, and again with his wife and children in 1938, 1948, and 1956, returning each time to his home in America.

———❧———

THE DEFENCE ACT, ACT NO 44 OF 1957

The Suppression of Communism Act; The Public Safety Act, 1953: Media Emergency Regulations; The Customs and Excise Act of 1955; The Official Secrets Act, Act No 16 of 1956; The Police Act, Act No 7 of 1958; The Prisons Act, Act No 8 of 1959; Publications and Entertainment Act of 1963; The Criminal Procedure Act, Act No 51 of 1977; The Publications Control Act, Act No 42 of 1974; The Internal Security Act, Act No 74 of 1982; The Protection of Information Act, Act No 84 of 1982; The Registration of Newspapers Amendment Act, Act No 98 of 1982.

All of these Acts, and others not listed here, placed severe constraints on the Press. The "English" Press was blamed for international condemnation of South Africa's apartheid policies. After Sharpeville, in 1960, the Prime Minister, Dr. H. Verwoerd, proclaimed in a radio address:

"A politically nonconformist Press will not be tolerated in the Republic."

THE GAGGING WRITS

Censorship is part of the fabric of life in South Africa. The government established a Board of Censors to censor books, films and other materials imported into or produced in South Africa. A wide variety of practices (both legal and extra-legal) combine to ensure that the articulation of certain facts and opinions are curtailed and prohibited. The weekly lists of publications which are banned under the Publications Act 42 of 1974 bear adequate testimony to the efficiency and productivity of our censors.

This is censorship in its extreme form: an institutionalized system by which films, books, plays and even objects, are banned by the State authority. But censorship in South Africa is infinitely more pervasive. Many statutes prohibit altogether the publication of certain information.

One of the more bizarre prohibitions was the one which prevented the publication of "any blank space or any obliteration or deletion of part of the text of a report or of a photograph" if such space indicated that it was intended to be understood as a reference to the effect of the censorship regulations. [Gilbert Marcus, *Reality*][49]

HIDING OUR SNICKERS

Our Lawyers Tell Us We Can Say Almost Nothing Critical about the Emergency. But We'll Try

The *Weekly Mail* proceeded to use black lines not only on this front page and in articles in this edition, but in articles in several subsequent editions as well ... This ingenious tactic actually accomplished several important objectives.

First, it was a means of revealing information that would not otherwise have been revealed. Rather than killing an article completely, or reframing it so that it essentially conveyed nothing, the process of keeping the original copy with only sections missing allowed readers to acquire a considerable amount of information...

The brief article, "Journalist ███████," provides an example in which it was possible to determine the blacked-out words. It reads as follows:

"Three journalists and photographers who regularly contribute to the *Weekly Mail* are among those ██████ under Emergency regulations. They are ██████ a Port Elizabeth reporter, ████████ and ████████ both Afrapix photographers from Johannesburg.

Also ████████ are two people who have been responsible for *Weekly Mail* distribution.

Given that this article appeared when the government was detaining literally thousands of individuals under the recently declared state of emergency, it is fairly obvious that the blacked-out word in the title, as well as in the text of the article, is "detained." ...[B]y publishing the article in this manner, the *Weekly Mail* was nevertheless able to convey the fact that individuals who regularly contributed to their newspaper had in fact been seized by the police. [Bryan Trabold, *College English*][50]
[Reprinted by permission, National Council of the Teachers of English]

NADINE GORDIMER on the Publications and Entertainment Act of 1963

"All this—intellectual isolation, isolation of ignorance among white people about the inner life of their countrymen of another color—this is the blunting of human faculties that control of communication is steadily achieving. It is essential to the maintenance of apartheid as a whole. We cannot expect to free ourselves of censorship, to bring life back to our numbed human responses, while apartheid lasts." [Nadine Gordimer, *Reality*][51]

ROBIN HALLETT ON BANNED BOOKS

You in South Africa have accepted a system of censorship which seems to [be] an insult and an affront to any intelligent man. I find it preposterous that the work of some of the most distinguished South African writers is not legally allowed to be read by their compatriots. I find it aggravating in the extreme that in teaching African Affairs I am not allowed to recommend to my students the handiest reference book that I know—*The Penguin Africa Handbook*. I do not know exactly why this book has been banned. I suppose, it contains a quotation from Luthuli or Mandela, or else its editor, a distinguished English journalist of South African origin, has fallen foul of your government for one reason or another. [Robin Hallett, *Reality*][52]

CENSORSHIP

All works which violate the rigid moral code of the Calvinist Dutch Reformed Church, all works which contradict the race theories of the Nationalist government ... are automatically excluded from South Africa under the Customs Act as soon as they come to the knowledge of the censors. Anyone who imports or is found knowingly in possession of any banned publication is liable to a fine of £1,000 or imprisonment for five years or both.

Sometimes censorship exceeds the bounds of all sense. The famous [black] trumpeter Louis Armstrong was excised altogether from *The Glen Miller Story*, although advertisements containing his name appeared all over the country. The advertising posters of *The King and I* were designed to show Deborah Kerr embraced by a bare-chested Yul Brynner in the role of a Siamese King. Since Siamese are Asians, however, this could not be allowed, and the posters were altered to reveal Deborah Kerr in the arms of a raceless shadow. [Subry Govander, *The Journalist*][53]

Advance was banned
The Guardian was banned
Africa South was banned
Spark was closed down
Fighting Talk was banned
New Age was banned
The World and *The Weekend World*, the only two newspapers respected among black people were banned
The Union of Black journalists was banned

Editors and journalists were harassed, arrested, imprisoned, tortured, detained without trial, banned, and exiled.

CHAPTER 16

SCHOOL DAYS: DURBAN GIRLS COLLEGE

What is it about school days that resonates so strongly—is it the sound of the bell, the sharp clap of a hockey stick as it hits the ball, or the thrice-repeated "hip-hip hooray for the holidays" at the end of each term? Perhaps it's the smell of fresh green paint on the walls, or the sound of the headmistress's feet as she walks down the corridor. Memories of Durban Girls College include all these things.

The province of Natal (now Kwa-Zulu Natal), on the East coast of South Africa, was a British enclave. Many of the girls in my school had grandparents or other family members living in England. Their mothers often talked about going "home," and they referred to Europe as "the continent," where it was traditional for children of wealthy Natal families to go on a European tour after completing high school. The British feel of the school, with its pervasive militaristic attitude, was something like a hangover from the Second World War.

Durban Girls College is a private school, founded in 1877 as *The Durban Young Ladies Collegiate Institution*. There were 500 girls from primary grades to matriculation when I was there. Our school uniforms were made of dark green Tobralco cotton, "bottle green," they called it, with white collar and cuffs and white buttons. Underneath, we wore matching green cotton bloomers, with elastic at the waist and legs, which our mothers had to sew for us. Our winter uniform consisted of a light woolen jumper with a white shirt. When it was cold, we wore a dark green woolen beret and blazer. Older girls wore black stockings with seams up the back, and sturdy, black laced shoes. Wearing makeup to school was forbidden, as was dyed or permanently waved hair. I used to curl mine, just enough to make a pretty pony tail, but I was called out of line one day and told I'd have to cut my hair if it prevented my hat from sitting at the right angle on my head.

Rachel in school uniform, Durban, Natal, 1952

It was against the rules to have pierced ears—only "common" girls had their ears pierced. Many of the girls who attended the Catholic school across the road, Maris Stella, had pierced ears. Jeannette recalls that the girls' nickname for Maris Stella girls was "Marie biscuits."

She has a prejudice against pierced ears to this day. If we pushed the sleeves of our sweaters up to our elbows, our teachers told us we looked like washerwomen. Sitting at your desk, you must keep your knees together, and girls were to keep the seams of their stockings straight at all times.

Boys' schools permitted the prefects (student council members) to cane younger boys for even minor infractions, like not knowing the names of the "cricket 13." When Mike was caned once, I can remember how upset mother was at the sight of those cruel red and blue welts. Dad wanted to march off to the school and confront whoever was responsible. Pehr once participated in a prank at school: he rigged up a sign that said "Larf" (laugh) that was attached to a string he let down every time the Latin master turned his back. The elderly teacher never figured out what was so funny. Boys were required to participate in "cadets," a military training exercise, which I have since learned was a plan of the Nationalist government to have all the boys ready to join the defense force. The government granted dual citizenship to foreign residents. If we hadn't left the country when we did, Mike could have been drafted. Girls didn't suffer the same sort of corporal punishment. Our Latin teacher, Miss Cross, the only Afrikaans-born mistress we had, used to swat girls' hands with a ruler, but she also threw mint candies at her pupils, just to get their attention.

I had to sit outside on a bench on the first day of school one term because I didn't have my quarantine certificate, an official document signed by the doctor confirming whether you had suffered an infectious disease during the holidays, and/or whether you were no longer contagious if you had been sick. I wasn't allowed inside until mother brought the missing document. The only vaccination we had in those days was for smallpox. Vaccination for the polio virus was started while I was in elementary school. In 1955, during a particularly severe polio epidemic, the newspapers carried frightening pictures of children in iron lungs. It was hard to imagine how uncomfortable that would be. The school required each of us to bring a towel from home as there were no paper towels or electric hand dryers, just linen roller towels that you pulled down, hoping to find a clean spot to dry your hands. During the epidemic we weren't allowed to swim at Durban's South

Beach, either: it was close to where the city sewer emptied into the sea. Sewage was considered as a possible source of the polio virus. Besides, the nurses at Addington Hospital, which was near the beach, were suffering from something they called "the mystery disease," perhaps a variant of the poliomyelitis virus.

Ocean swimming carried another deadly predator: sharks. Sharks frequent the Natal sea coast, especially during the sardine runs, when they gather in large numbers. As Durban grew as a popular tourist destination, tales of shark attacks led to the installation of shark nets. The surprising thing about those nets is that they run parallel to the coast but are open at either end. The Natal Sharks Board scientists, experts in the habits of sharks, explained that sharks swim in a zig-zag pattern, so many of them are actually caught on the *inside* of the net. Swimming at unprotected beaches is not encouraged. There was a sad incident where a promising young pianist lost a hand to a shark attack when swimming down the south coast, where there were no nets.

At Durban Girls College, students had to go everywhere in lines: up the stairs, down the halls, out to the bus stop, marching into morning prayers, everywhere. The shortest was always first, the tallest at the back. I was the shortest pupil in my class for most of my school years. Every morning we lined up and filed (silently) into the big school Hall where morning prayers were conducted by the headmistress. We sang English hymns like *All Things Bright and Beautiful* and *Jerusalem the Golden* from little blue hymn books. I began to think that Jerusalem must be in England. After prayers, we were greeted with a hearty, "Good morning, gels." We were expected to reply with enthusiastic vigor, or we'd have to say it again, "Good morning, Miss Christison!"

In music class, we sang songs like *Flow Gently, Sweet Avon*; *The British Grenadiers*; and *D'ye Ken John Peel?* an English hunting song with a rousing refrain, "with his hounds and his horn in the morning." The United Kingdom of England, Scotland, and Wales was well-represented: we sang about the Scots Bonnie Prince Charlie and learned the spirited Welsh military song, *Men of Harlech*, commemorating a fifteenth-century seven-year siege. It was a relief to sing *Waltzing Matilda* in honor of our sister colony, Australia, though we didn't know what a billabong was. The words to these songs must have had little meaning to most of us young girls in the South Africa of the 1950s.

When the young English princess Elizabeth was crowned Queen in June of 1953, there were celebrations throughout South Africa, and every school child was given a Coronation cup, a gold-rimmed mug bearing the likeness of the young Queen. There was an old mansion in Durban known as "the King's house," because visiting royalty stayed there when they graced the colony with their presence. It was surrounded by an iron fence and lots of trees, so you could barely catch a glimpse of it, but that only added to the fascination the British royalty held for the colonials.

We studied the usual variety of subjects. Like my sister Kirstin, I loved botany class. We learned about the parts of an azalea flower: the sticky stigma, the pistil, the pollen-bearing anthers, and the stamens. We drew clematis flowers and seed pods. We studied geography and history—South African and English history. I didn't learn any American history until I returned to America. Kirstin reported that her teacher referred to the American Revolution as "The War of Independence."

Deportment was an important topic—we were constantly reminded to stand or sit up straight. This aspect of our physical education was handled by the gym teacher. There was even a prize for best deportment. In my class, Eve always won that prize. Out of doors, we played hockey, tennis, and netball, and we wore thick woolen swimming costumes (swimsuits) for swimming class.

At the end of the sophomore year in high school, Fourth Form (or Standard Eight), students were required to sit for the Junior Certificate, the JC, a state exam set by the Province of Natal. Sixth Form students, seniors, took the Matriculation exam. These state exams were grueling, three-hour ordeals. Passing "Matric" with high marks was necessary for going on to university. Essays were required, never one-word answers or "fill in the blanks." Hardly anyone earned an A, which was 80 to 100 percent. The state required certain "set books" for the English literature exam. Each year there was a different Shakespeare play on the required syllabus: We read *The Merchant of Venice* the year I sat for the Junior Certificate.

I suffered from being the third member of our family to attend the school. My math teacher once wondered aloud why I couldn't do math like my older sisters, while I stood there in front of my classmates, humiliated. I remember asking Jeannette if she were really that good at math. My sister Kirstin was "Dux of the school" the year she graduated. The student with the highest grades was named Dux, Latin for "leader," and her name was engraved for posterity on a huge wooden and brass plaque outside the headmistress's office.

After my JC year, I left Durban Girls College and attended the Natal Technical College to bridge the six months between the end of my Sophomore year in South Africa and the start of Junior year in America. Mother believed that all her daughters should learn how to type, and this was her chance with me. I took typing and cooking, dressmaking, and flower arranging, among other less-useful things, like hat-making.

Going to school in South Africa was traumatic for the older children in the family, who had started their school days in the gentler American public schools of Montclair, New Jersey. It was similarly uncomfortable for me when I had to adjust to a different school culture after returning to America. I felt acutely uncomfortable by the more relaxed behavior of both students and teachers—I was frequently on edge, waiting for someone to be called out and sent to the principal's office. But I have always been grateful for my good, solid British schooling. It has served me well.

———————

THE NATIVES LAWS AMENDMENT ACT OF 1957

Association by Permission
The implications of the Bill ... are far-reaching. The Minister of Native Affairs, may, with the concurrence of the local authority, "prohibit the holding of any meeting, assembly, or gathering (including any social gathering), which is attended by any Native, in any urban area outside of a Native residential area," if he considers such a meeting is likely to

cause a nuisance, or likely to be undesirable having regard to the locality in which the premises are situated. And he may by notice to any person, prohibit that person from holding or organizing or arranging such meeting.

If any person disobeys a law by way of protest, he may be sentenced to three years' imprisonment or £300 fine or ten lashes or any two of these, and if he organized such protest, to five years or £500 fine or ten lashes or any two of these. [Alan Paton, *Africa South*][54]

FUNERALS

Funerals have received special attention by the authorities. A grotesque cycle of death has arisen in South Africa with many deaths at police hands occurring at funerals. Because of extensive prohibitions on the holding of meetings, funerals have become one of the few outlets for political speech. The clamps on the holding of funerals have been particularly severe. Typical conditions prohibit the holding of funerals out of doors. Only ordained ministers of religion are allowed to speak at such funerals and flags, banners, placards, pamphlets or posters cannot be displayed or distributed. There is usually a restriction on the number of persons allowed to attend a funeral and the duration of funerals is also generally restricted. [*Reality*][55]

CHAPTER 17

A POLYGLOT NATION: THE AFRIKAANS FARM

South Africa was a bilingual country when we lived there: English and Afrikaans were the official languages. Ironically, black Africans were eventually schooled only in Afrikaans, because the government didn't want them to get any ideas about "rising above their status of a laboring class." The Afrikaans language was an important unifying factor for the Dutch Boer population. The government had also sought to spread Afrikaans culture "fostering patriotism and national pride," by holding national festivals and erecting monuments to Afrikaans Voortrekker (pioneer) heroes.[56] Our school took part in a folkdance festival. Mother made a special skirt for me to wear for that event: it flared out when I twirled around to the reedy sound of traditional Boer (farmer) music played on an accordion, or concertina.

South African English carries hints of the many cultures that have added their "spice" to the language: African languages, including San Bushman; Portuguese traders; Dutch settlers; Malay; Indian; British, and others. Now there are eleven official languages: Afrikaans, English, Ndebele, Northern Sotho, Sotho, Swazi, Tsonga, Tswana, Venda, Xhosa, and Zulu.

Our school was an English school, but we were required to learn Afrikaans, and we were supposed to speak only Afrikaans on Tuesdays. It was amusing to listen to our very British headmistress stumble through morning prayers in a language she clearly was unfamiliar with. Schools did not teach African languages, though my brother Pehr studied Zulu when he went to college. He became so fluent that he was written up in the newspaper. We loved to hear him say a sentence that contained all the clicks in the Zulu language, and he loved to show it off, too.

The state exams we sat at the end of the tenth and twelfth grades included an Afrikaans Language exam. Some students took advantage of extra practice by going to an Afrikaans farm, or *boetplaas,* in the October Michaelmas holidays. My brother Michael and both my older sisters and I were treated to this uniquely South African experience.

I was accompanied by one of my schoolmates, Anna. We were excited. It was the first time either of us had been away from our families. We met at the cavernous, echoing South African Railways Station, across from the Durban flower market. Pigeons swooped under the rafters; steam hissed from the underbellies of the big black coal-burning engines, and African porters called out to each other from either side of the tracks as they wheeled creaking wooden barrows piled high with suitcases. When we found our compartment in the train, we leaned out of the window to wave goodbye to our parents, just the way they do in the movies. Anna was taller than I am. Like me, she also had red hair and freckles. Her family was from Scotland. There were boys on the train, too. It's just as well our parents weren't aware of that—Anna let one of them kiss her!

Our destination was in the Orange Free State, on the other side of the Drakensberg. The province was originally settled by Dutch Boer farmers as the Boer Republic, in an effort to escape British rule at the Cape, but it was lost to the British in the Boer War and incorporated by the Union of South Africa. The train, known affectionately as the "milk train," travelled all night, stopping at little towns all along the way. At bedtime, the smartly dressed porter pulled down the upper bunks and made them up with starched white sheets and thick green wool blankets embossed with the logo of the South African Railways.

Women got dressed up to travel in the 1950s, so there we were: two fifteen-year old girls in dresses, nylon stockings, and little high heels (called "baby Louis" heels)—definitely no blue jeans or athletic shoes. When we arrived at our destination the next morning, we left the train at the railroad depot and climbed onto a splintery wooden wagon, prickly with leftover hay, pulled by a large, old tractor. (That was the end of the nylon stockings.) The driver stopped to deliver the boys at the first farmhouse we came to, and the girls were taken on down the bumpy unpaved track to the main farmhouse. There we were met by the farmer's wife, whom we were to address as *Mevrouw,* meaning Madam, or Missus.

Mevrouw never spoke a word of English to us for ten days, and she expected us to obey the same rule: no English. She stationed little African girls outside our bedroom doors who were to listen and report to her on any infractions. Anna and I were fortunate in that our bedroom was a little rondavel, separate from the main farmhouse. A school friend, Adele, shared it with us. I suspect that her well-to-do parents had arranged it. We used a lot of sign language and became experts at soundless whispering. We didn't know what punishment was planned for anyone heard speaking English, and we didn't want to find out.

All the girls were expected to be at their desks in the schoolroom at six a.m. sharp, dressed—unexpectedly—in our pajamas, slippers, and warm bathrobes. Perhaps Mevrouw thought we would take too long to get dressed? The Free State is located on a high plateau, so it was cold in the early mornings, even in October. We drank big mugs full of steaming hot tea while Mevrouw drilled us in Afrikaans grammar. This morning mental exercise was calculated to wake us up, which was hard on the girls who had climbed out their windows the night before to meet the boys in the fields. After morning class, we dressed and joined Mevrouw and her family for a big farm breakfast. My sister Jeannette says the food was awful, but I don't remember—I was too afraid of Mevrouw to think about what I was eating. If you wanted some butter and couldn't ask for it in Afrikaans, you ate without it. Her husband, the farmer, joined us at the table at dinner time and tried to conduct an intelligent conversation with us. The boys came over to join us for class during the day.

Before we left to return home, we were invited to a barbecue or *braaivleis* at the boys' farm, where they served *boerewors*, spicy Afrikaans farmers' sausage. Michael says Dad and Mother would never have let us go to that farm if they had known what the farmer was really like. He spoke of women in derogatory terms and expected the boys to laugh with him. The extra practice must have helped because I passed the examination.

Living in a bilingual country that was still part of the British Commonwealth, we sang two national anthems: *God Save the King—God Save the Queen* after 1953, when Queen Elizabeth II was crowned—and *Die Stem*, the Afrikaans anthem. Nowadays, the hymn, *'Nkosi Sikelel'* iAfrika' (God bless Africa), which became a song of protest during the long fight against apartheid, is sung first in several African languages, followed by the first verse of *Die Stem* in Afrikaans, and finally, the last verse is sung in English. I cannot sing *'Nkosi Sikele* without tears. We once recorded my father singing it. He loved it too, and sang it beautifully with his full bass voice, especially the words *Woza Moya*, "Come Holy Spirit," which were among the original words to the song.

Nkosi sikelel' iAfrika

	Nkosi sikelel' iAfrika	God bless Africa
Xhosa	*Maluphakanyisw' uphondo lwayo*	Let its (Africa's) horn be raised,
	Yizwa imithandazo yethu	Listen also to our prayers.
Zulu	*Nkosi sikelela, thina lusapho lwayo*	Lord bless us, we are the family of it (Africa)
	Morena boloka setjhaba sa heso	Lord bless our nation
	O fedise dintwa le matshwenyeho	Stop wars and sufferings,
Sotho	*O se boloke, O se boloke setjhaba sa heso,*	Save it, save our nation,
	Setjhaba sa, South Afrika, South Afrika.	The nation of South Africa, South Africa.
Afrikaans	*Uit die blou van onse hemel,*	From the blue of our skies,
	Out die diepte van onse see,	From depth of our sea,
	Oor onse ewige gebergtes,	Over everlasting mountains,
	Waar die kranse antwoord gee,	Where the cliffs give answer,
English	*Sounds the call to come together, And united we shall stand*	
	Let us live and strive for freedom In South Africa, our land.	

The Soweto Student Uprising

In June 1976, the school children of Soweto rose in protest against Bantu Education, provoked by the imposition in schools of that symbol of oppression, the Afrikaans language. Police shot dead Hector Petersen, 13 years old, and many other children. The protest broadened to one against the whole apartheid system.

From Soweto, demonstrations swept the county. In sixteen months, there were 700 publicly recorded deaths, mainly young people shot by police. Hundreds of school children were taken into detention, some were still in detention 18 months later, and some were never seen again by their families. [Mary Benson, *anc.org.za*][57]

Interview with Winnie Mandela by Eric Abraham

Abraham: According to an eyewitness report in the initial incident in Soweto the police fired first and the stones were thrown afterwards. Do you believe this to be correct, or do you have any further information as to who started the confrontation?

Mandela: I happened to be present. I was on the scene, I was, however, not present when the first shots were fired at the children. What happened was that as the about 10,000 children marched towards the Orlando West High School—where they intended to hold an innocent meeting at which they were going to formulate a strategy in the event of the department compelling [them] to continue with the Afrikaans [as the language of instruction] ... So what happened as they were nearing the school, the police fired at the innocent schoolchildren who were right in front, these children were aged between 8 and 10 years.

These children were not even part of the demonstration. The first shots landed on a boy of about 10 years old.

Abraham: So all indications are that the response on the part of the schoolchildren was provoked by the excessive measures used by the police?

Mandela: Yes, of course. What the police did was to set a dog on the child. The dog bit the child and the students naturally got hold of the dog to protect the child and as they did that, this particular policeman fired the first shots at this child, who died on the spot. That is how the dog got killed, and that is how they provoked 10,000 children. [Winnie Mandela, *Wits Historical Papers*][58]

CHAPTER 18

BUNZEE

I came across Bunzee one day at noon. He was squatting on the sun-warmed tiles outside Mother's study, the room we all called the library because there were bookcases along two walls filled with the books Mother had brought from America. Mother had told me to leave him alone to eat his lunch in peace, but that day I had just happened to be coming along the side of the house, and there he was.

Bunzee worked in our garden. He cut the grass, slowly, with hand-held clippers. He refused to use the push mower. He wore a dirty white rag wound about and knotted on the top of his head. I don't know if he had any hair. He was very thin, his face wizened, and he rarely spoke to anybody. He had brought his lunch with him, wrapped in some newspaper which he spread out on the tile to serve as a plate. It was curry, strong-smelling, yellow, the color of mustard. He ate with his hands, but he had very few teeth so he mashed the food around in his mouth.

Bunzee was a Hindu. South Africans called Indians "Coolies." There was considerable discrimination against Indians, and anything to do with them. They were from the untouchable class, we were told, and were "not to be trusted," they would be sure to cheat you somehow. Bunzee would never have been accepted to eat lunch with our Zulu servants or with us.

In the middle of the nineteenth century, lower caste Indians were brought to South Africa to work as indentured labor on the sugar farms in Natal, up the north coast from Durban. They had a hard time working for the British in India, and then for the South Africans during apartheid. Promises regarding citizenship and land ownership were not kept, and indigenous Africans were not happy with them because of a feeling that they took jobs.

Bunzee asked if he could plant a row of hot pepper plants along the path beside the tennis court. Dad said that would be fine, as long as they didn't cross-pollinate with his green pepper plants. Peppers were called capsicum. Well, of course, they did cross-pollinate. Dad did not care for hot peppers. He was not happy with Bunzee.

When we first moved to Durban, the Indian vegetable sellers used to come around to the houses in our neighborhood. Men and women carried their heavy, produce-laden baskets balanced at the ends of long poles that were carefully centered on matted rags on their bony shoulders. The woven grass baskets bounced up and down as they walked along. The Indian women wore saris and had magenta circles painted in the middle of their foreheads. The fruit and vegetables, warmed from the sun, let off a ripe, musky odor which, combined with the scent of the woven grass basket, I have never forgotten.

A year after we arrived in South Africa, there were what was referred to as "race riots" in Durban. The trouble was between the Africans and the Indians. Stores were looted and burned, over a hundred people were killed, and thousands injured. The Africans were protesting unfair treatment in that Indians had the monopoly over economic resources, trading rights, and ownership of property that they could not themselves obtain. The Afrikaner government seized upon this idea to emphasize the importance of the division of all South Africans by race and they embarked upon a period of comprehensive segregation and security legislation.

My sister Jeannette recounts how one night during the race riots there were a lot of loud shouts out on the sidewalk near our house. Our African maid, Sophie, brought an injured Indian man into the back room near the kitchen. He hid under the table, afraid that someone would follow him inside. Mother coaxed him out and gestured to him to sit in one of the dining chairs so she could attend to his knife wounds, but he wouldn't sit. He said he couldn't sit in the presence of a white woman. When they were sure there was no more disturbance on the street, they let the man go. It must have been a difficult and frightening beginning to the family's sojourn in Durban.

Mahatma Gandhi lived in Durban for many years. It was there that he practiced law and developed his doctrine of peaceful resistance. Gandhi learned from history that dictators, regardless of their geographic origin, cleverness, wealth, fame, or brutality, in the end always fall:

> *When I despair, I remember that all through history the way of truth and love have always won. There have been tyrants and murderers and, for a time, they can seem invincible, but in the end, they always fall. Think of it, always.*[59]
>
> Mahatma Gandhi

⟶⊰●⊱⟵

"THE GHETTO ACT" OR THE ASIATIC LAND TENURE AND INDIAN REPRESENTATION ACT, ACT NO 28 OF 1946 AMENDED IN 1952 AND 1956

Prohibited Indians from owning property outside of certain designated areas.

The Ghetto Act

The Indian people, considered to be "a foreign and an outlandish element," must be uprooted and expatriated. They must be isolated in ghettoes, their wealth destroyed, properties confiscated and means of livelihood taken away ... By relegating the non-White people to ghettoes and by subjecting them to rigid control, it would be [possible] to swell the ranks of cheap labour. [Yusuf Cachalia, *Africa South*][60]

GENOCIDE! SOPHIATOWN INDIANS FORCED OUT OF SHOPS, HOMES

JOHANNESBURG

Indian families who have lived in Sophiatown for as long as 30 and 40 years were forced to move to Lenasia. Some families have had to move from 5 and 6-roomed houses into a single-roomed hut without partitions or ceilings. Toilets and other amenities have to be shared. Others were waiting in their homes with their possessions packed but were unable to afford the £5 asked by the removal lorries ... Their shops were closed down, "All our life's savings."

Critically ill, Mr. P. has decided not to leave. Lenasia is miles away from the nearest doctor and there is no hospital nearby. His doctor told him he would not attend him if he moves to Lenasia. He was turned down by the Group Areas Settlement ... who refused to grant him an extension. [*New Age*][61]

CHAPTER 19

A LESSON IN COURAGE: CLIMBING WITH MY BROTHER

If you plan a longer hike into the high mountain wilderness of the Drakensberg, you are required to register your route at the hotel office and give an estimate of your expected return date. There was no way to communicate to or from the mountains in those days, so rescue parties were sent out to find any climbers who didn't return within a reasonable length of time. In the 1950s, rangers had to carry injured people out of the mountains to safety. It was very difficult, and often dangerous. Nowadays, stranded or injured climbers are picked up by rescue teams in helicopters. The slap-slap of the helicopter blades echoes against the mountainside.

One time when Pehr desperately wanted to join some school friends on a climbing expedition, Mother and Dad refused to let him go. The route they were planning was considered too dangerous. As it happened, we were hiking down Verkykerskop when we met this very group of young men on their way up to the contour path. We were horrified to hear shortly afterwards that one of the party was bitten by a berg adder when he went to get some water from the stream after dark. He died before aid could reach him.

We liked climbing Verkykerskop (which means "look-out mountain" in Afrikaans), but there were troops of baboons in the cliffs, some of them quite large: the leading male would move out in front of his troop, bark in a threatening way, and make bluffing charges. Pehr just threw a stone in their direction to scare them away, but I was afraid they might block the path coming back down, and then what would we do? Baboons are smart. The forest ranger, Mr. Boekler, said that if they were getting "cheeky, they needed to be kept in line." Mike remembers his saying that he would "go up and shoot some of them."

About half way up Verkykerskop, hikers usually stop at a sparkling waterfall, Sterkspruit Falls. The water in the mountain streams of the Drakensberg is crystal clear and very cold. Here, where the cascading water forms a pool edged by rocks, trees, dripping moisture, provide shade, their damp trunks appearing black in the misty gloom. It is the perfect spot to sit down, remove your shoes and socks, and gratefully dip hot, tired feet in the water until they tingle with the cold. If the falls were our destination that day, we ate a picnic lunch before going back down; at other times we climbed higher, to reach the contour path on the plateau. From there you can see all around, miles of rolling veld in front and, behind you, the towering peaks.

The mountains of the dragon, Drakensberg, Natal, 1952

Pehr loved those mountains so much it was contagious. He enjoyed wilderness areas wherever he could find them. We all looked up to him: he had such an interesting, adventurous life. There was his knowledge of the mountains; his trip up the Congo River on a riverboat; a visit to Tree Tops Inn in Kenya, where the elephants come and scratch their backs against the tree trunks that hold up the building. He even travelled to Pago Pago in American Samoa to visit an isolated member of the church who lived there. His love of old trees took him to northern Pennsylvania to see the old growth trees in the State Forests, the "forest medieval," as he called them. And he loved taking long walks to see the indigenous yellowwood trees that grew in the forested ravines of the Drakensberg. Real yellowwood [podocarpus] is South Africa's National Tree.

Fearless, he would set off by himself in his well-worn suede veldskoens (suede hiking boots), old khaki shorts, and crushed cotton bush hat, his canvas knapsack slung over a shoulder, a stout walking stick in his hand. He was careful to have the snakebite kit up-to-date, and he taught us all what to do if someone were bitten. (That protocol has since changed. Now the experts tell you *not* to cut the skin around the bite, and *not* to suck out the venom or place a tourniquet on an arm or leg above the bite.) Pehr wasn't scared away by the baboon's bark or the laugh of a hyena in the bush. I so much wanted to be brave like him.

About that hyena: it was not one of my best moments, as they say. We had set out on a long day's hike up into the Little Berg, a long range of high foothills. Pehr wanted to share one of his favorite wild places with us, a place he had named the Yellowwood Forest. He told us how the maidenhair ferns with dainty black stems, which Mother particularly loved, grow along the banks of the stream. About halfway through the morning when we stopped for a rest, there was a puff adder, sunning itself on the outcrop of rocks just where we were about to sit. Puff adders are slow-moving, venomous snakes, with long fangs that inflict a painful, poisonous bite. After Pehr had chased it away, we sat and enjoyed the view: the heat and dust clouds hid the horizon, but somewhere down there was the sea, miles and miles away.

I was already nervous because of the snake when we heard the bark—or was it a laugh? "It must be a baboon," someone said. Then

Pehr made his usual mistake of suggesting the worst, "It sounds like a hyena." This large carnivore makes a sort of giggle, a warning sound, when afraid. I was not interested in seeing a hyena. Hyenas bring up thoughts of sharp teeth and claws. With its sloping body, from shoulder to tail, a hyena looks something like a large, misshapen dog, and it can run very fast. My brothers tried to downplay the fact that it might be a hyena. Dad was not so sure. I was not going to believe that the insane, human-sounding laugh coming from a nearby hill was not a hyena, so we turned around and started home. It's small wonder Pehr liked to put his colds hands around my neck! I had ruined his special outing.

Fisi, the Hyena, was one of the funniest animals of all in Geraldine Elliot's book, *The Long Grass Whispers*. Fisi was portrayed as a comical, vain sort of a fellow. The stories are very entertaining, passed on down by grandmothers of the Ngoni tribe. My father likened them to *Uncle Remus*. The characters, such as Kalulu the Hare and Kamba the Tortoise, reveal the almost human personality traits of individual wild animals. Dad would laugh and laugh as he read, and we all laughed with him.

Not long before the encounter with the hyena's laugh, we found a set of large paw prints in the sand outside the girls' bedroom window. Much to Mother's irritation, Pehr suggested it might have been a leopard—as I have said, he was good at coming up with the most dire explanations that invariably scared me. Leopards are stealthy nocturnal hunters so I insisted on closing the bedroom window at night after that, even in hot weather. After all, that window was right beside the head of my own bed. My brother Michael, well known for playing devil's advocate, tried to reassure me that it was "just a big dog."

I never believed that story about a big dog. Mike overheard Dad asking the game ranger if it could have been a leopard. "Leopards have been seen in the mountains," he said, "and they do hunt at night, but it would be unusual for one of the big cats to come down so close to humans." He warned us that our open trash pit might attract animals.

Before we left South Africa to return to America, Pehr promised to take me on a hike up to the contour path, just the two of us. He checked to see if we had everything we needed, and we were ready to go. He hooked his blue enameled billycan to the side of his canvas knapsack—it clinked merrily in rhythm to his step as he walked along. Walking sticks in hand, we headed up Verkykerskop to the contour path on the plateau, Pehr slowing his usual fast pace to meet my shorter stride. Midway, at Sterkspruit Falls, he filled the billycan with the water we would use for our lunch. We built a little fire out of sticks when we reached the contour path and put the billycan on the flames. When the water was boiling, he stirred in an envelope of dried chicken noodle soup. There, up in the mountains he loved so much, we shared the best cup of soup I have ever tasted. I felt so grown up being on the mountain with him, just the two of us. Maybe I even gained some of his courage.

Pehr's knapsack and walking stick, Drakensberg, Natal, 1952

General Laws Amendment Act, Act No 76 of 1962 (Sabotage Act)

For the first time, the death sentence could be used for acts of sabotage.

This Act increased the state president's power to declare organisations unlawful and to add further restrictions to banning orders. It defined sabotage and made provision for a minimum sentence of five years and a maximum sentence of death.... Hundreds of South African Congress of Trade Union (SACTU) members fell victims of this Act. Their detention period ranged from 90 to 180 days. Those found guilty were imprisoned, some in solitary confinement, and sometimes tortured. Lots of people lost their lives and a campaign was launched to free those languishing in jail due to the act. [*South African History Online*][62]

House Arrest and the Rule of Law

In October, the Minister of Justice, Mr. B. J. Vorster, exercised powers conferred upon him by the **General Laws Amendment Act** and issued the first House Arrest Order, which confined a Johannesburg woman to her home at night and at week-ends and on public holidays for a period of five years. [Hon. O.D. Schreiner, *The Black Sash*][63]

Helen Joseph was placed under house arrest (some called it civil death) for five years by the Minister of Justice. Detectives called on her at all hours of the day, just to check that she was there... The Special Branch detectives ... sat in cars outside her house every night for an hour or two. One day they searched her entire house and garden to

188

make sure she was alone. When her banning was lifted, she could not make any public disclaimer against [the reason for her house arrest], because no statement or utterance of a banned person may be published or circulated. "We are thus unable to speak in our own defense." [Helen Joseph, *Tomorrow's Sun*][64]

Helen Joseph was awarded the ANC's highest award, the Isitwalandwe/Seaparankoe Medal, for her devotion to the liberation struggle as a symbol of defiance, integrity and courage. [*South African History Online*][65]

MASS PROTEST BY UNIVERSITY STAFFS IN NATAL ARRESTS WITHOUT TRIAL DENOUNCED

DURBAN, June 30, 1963. One hundred and eleven members of the academic staffs of the University of Natal in Durban and Pietermaritzburg have signed pledges to take strong action if any colleagues are detained or victimized under the **General Law Amendment Act**, which provides for detention up to 90 days without trial....

Silencing Teachers

The preamble to the pledges document expresses "determination to oppose with the strongest protest any further violations of academic freedom without which there can be no university education in the accredited meaning of that term." The statement adds that the Act may be used to silence university teachers who while innocent of any political crime may in the normal course of academic duties present views in conflict with the particular ideology of the government in power.... . Two Natal University students, both Africans, are among the more than 100 people at present under 90-day detention without trial.[66]

The Times / News Syndication

The General Laws Amendment Act of 1964 (passed in 1963), dubbed **the 90-Day Act** as it provides for any person to be detained, **without trial, for 90 days.** Further, on the expiration of such, the person could be re-arrested under the same law for another 90 days, a process this new law allows to be repeated indefinitely.

The Act also allows the state to retrospectively declare unlawful those organisations existing since 7 April 1960… In 1964, 671 people were charged with contravention of security laws and [Prime Minister] Vorster justifies this by declaring his actions necessary to protect the country against Communist conspiracy. [*South African History Online*][67]

CHAPTER 20

TRANSITION: RETURN TO AMERICA

It was truly a bittersweet moment when we left for America in 1960. There had been an escalation of racial unrest in South Africa at the time, and we were leaving our sister Jeannette behind. A few months before we were to leave, she married Johnny Botha [no relation to S. African President P. W. Botha]. They planned to make their home together in South Africa. Our brother Pehr would also stay behind, temporarily, to supervise the African church, but we were looking forward to seeing our sister Kirstin, who had remained in America in 1956. She had married the year before, and she and her husband Feodor had a baby girl, Naomi, the first grandchild—I was so proud to be an auntie.

The church was building a new house for us, a "colonial," with Williamsburg blue woodwork. The word "colonial" had a different meaning in America. We had seen architect's sketches—it was nothing like our home at 185 Sydenham Road. We were amazed by the attic and the cellar—houses in South Africa don't have these—and there was a garage where the car could park inside, under the house. Mike, Siri, and I got to choose the wallpaper and paint colors for our own bedrooms. I had never seen wallpaper before. It was fun to go through the book of swatches they had sent us.

We sailed in July, 1960, on the *Edinburgh Castle*, a steamship in the Union Castle Line. It was a two-week voyage from Durban to Southampton, England. In contrast to the *African Endeavor*, this British ship was strictly divided by class: first class, second class, and steerage. People from the lower classes were not allowed to go to certain decks or dining rooms reserved only for first class passengers. It was not as comfortable as the ships we had sailed on in 1956, and it was crowded: Siri and I shared our parents' small cabin. We slept on the top bunks and Mom and Dad had the lower ones. At least it had a port hole—Mike was in a windowless cabin with other young men he didn't know. When we wanted a bath, we made an appointment with the steward, who filled the tub to the top with steaming hot water—*salt* water. A jug of fresh water was provided for rinsing, not nearly enough to rinse the shampoo out of my long hair.

There was a group of young men from Southern Rhodesia (now Zimbabwe) on board the *Edinburgh Castle*. Dad didn't approve of my spending time with them and referred to them as "Rhodesian gorillas." More than once he came up on deck in the late evening, walking stick in hand, and fiercely commanded me to "come down to the cabin, right away." He worried about me and didn't want me mixing with that crowd, but I was very embarrassed at his behavior. He was right, I was completely naïve, not yet sixteen, and they were young (white) men in their twenties.

You might think a closed environment like a ship would help our parents keep control of us, but that was not so. Siri got lost by following a new friend to the first-class cabins, and I evaded Dad several times and visited the boys (and girls) down in the steerage cabins. There was a woman down there who kept an eye on us all. "No closed doors," she said, firmly. She taught us how to properly iron a man's shirt and trousers, a useful skill I was glad to have.

After the ship docked in Southampton we went to Holland for a few weeks, where Dad spent time with other church leaders. We stayed in a superb hotel in The Hague, the stately *Wittebrug*, where we ate beautifully cooked meals and walked in its lovely rose garden. In Holland they eat bread and cheese for breakfast, but you must not put butter on bread with cheese. And there was gingerbread with big sugar crystals on top. It was at the Wittebrug that I had my first taste of red wine. But I remember being upset with Mother, who was suddenly strict about my wearing lipstick—the Dutch people look down on women who wore makeup, she said.

After a brief stopover in London, we set sail for New York in August. The captain had chosen the northern Atlantic route, so it was a five-day voyage through grey and stormy weather. On Holland-Amerika's ship, the SS *Statendam*, the woman whose job it was to keep the children happy expected us teens to join in the games with little kids. Mike and I rebelled and refused to go with her. There were movies every night: one of them was *Splendor in the Grass*. Dad made Siri and me leave the movie theater, but Mike stayed behind. He was not going to let Dad tell him what to do. Again, we were embarrassed. That happened several times, until we gave up going to the movies.

This time of transition was hard. We were suddenly confronted by a lot of new experiences. I feel that our parents misjudged just how difficult it would be for us. They were going home to the place where they grew up. We were not used to American customs or American schools, and, unlike our parents, we didn't know anybody there other than our sister Kirstin. We were what they now call "Third Culture Kids," not completely at home in the country where we grew up, nor did we feel we belonged in our country of origin. I recently found some letters I wrote at that time. I was clearly bewildered. I felt that I didn't fit in. Others talked about TV shows I had never watched (we didn't have TV in South Africa), they would go about saying things like, "Scooby, dooby, do!" and my classmates, who were all a little older than me, were learning how to drive. You had to be twenty-one to get a driver's license in South Africa, not just sixteen. Some of the vocabulary they used confused me and resulted in great embarrassment. The American word rubber, slang for condom, means an eraser in South Africa, and the American word "movement," in reference to bodily waste, is "motion" where I grew up. I was elected to be secretary of the junior class shortly after I arrived at the high school, since I was considered exotic, I suppose. They told me to say, "I make a motion to ...." Horrified by the use of that word in this context, I changed it to, "I make a movement..." which was followed by a roar of laughter from the other students. When I delivered the valedictory speech at graduation they told me I sounded like Queen Elizabeth. It was some time before I lost my British South African accent.

When we sailed away from South Africa, we carried with us our clothes and furniture, and boxes full of books; the precious chain-stitching Wilcox and Gibbs sewing machine; and the dining room table that had belonged to Mother's Caldwell grandmother; but the real treasures stowed away on that ship with us were our memories. You don't grow out of your memories; they don't break or shatter or fall apart; they can't be eaten up by bookworms, or dry out in the tropical sun, but you can always work toward understanding them better.

THE SHARPEVILLE MASSACRE
21 MARCH, 1960

The pass book had become a major symbol for black resentment and resistance.

MASS SLAUGHTER BY POLICE
Bloody Reprisals Against Anti-Pass Demonstrators
The first day of the Pan Africanist campaign against passes brought frightful reprisals from the police in the areas where the people came out *en masse* in answer to the call to stay home from work and hand in their passes at the police station.

At Sharpeville Township and at Langa a total of 70 were killed and several hundreds wounded. The police firing was without any warning, some told New Age... This murderous shooting was done from behind a wire fence into the centre of the crowd standing about the police station. The police said, as justification, that they were being stoned and fired upon, but on their own admission only three police were injured that day. A police official pointed to scratched paintwork as evidence of stoning. [Joe Gqabi, *New Age*][68]

VILIFIED APARTHEID-ERA MINISTER DIES A HERO: DENOUNCED SEGREGATION. SHARPEVILLE WAS BEYERS NAUDE'S CRISIS OF FAITH

For 40 years, Beyers Naude [an ordained Dutch Reformed Church minister] lived as an outcast, persecuted because of his opposition to apartheid...He stood before the congregation of his church in Johannesburg and publicly denounced apartheid as immoral and un-Christian, condemning his own faith for its biblical justifications of white supremacism.

From 1977 to 1984, he was banned by the South African government... In 1990...he was the sole Afrikaner in an ANC delegation that opened peace talks with the government. [Peter Goodspeed, *National Post* (Canada)][69]

A STATE OF EMERGENCY

On the morning of March 30th, just over a week after the Sharpeville killings, a **State of Emergency** was declared in the Union of South Africa... From 2 a.m. on the morning of March 30th hundreds of people were arrested all over the country... The prisoners came from all walks of life, all income groups, all parts of the country, all political parties, both sexes. And the next day a Government Gazette Extraordinary officially declared a **State of Emergency** and announced that anyone could be arrested under it in the interests of public safety and order. [Alan Rake, *Africa South*][70]

STATE OF EMERGENCY EXTENDED TO 31 MORE DISTRICTS

CAPE TOWN, April 2, 1960

In Durban today the police opened fire on a column of Africans. Three were killed and three wounded. One of the dead was reported to be a woman. The shooting was in Berea Road, a main thoroughfare in a white residential area of the city. Heavily armed police have been patrolling the township of Cato Manor after reports that the situation in the township was tense.

The Times / News Syndication

OTHER GROUPS STOPPED
DURBAN, April 1, 1960

The shooting in Durban occurred when the column of Africans surged through the streets to the gaol to demand release of their leaders... The column marched along the main street in Durban. The marchers sang and shouted freedom slogans and forced African onlookers to swell their ranks.

The South African Press Association reported that the column caught the police and Europeans by surprise in an outflanking movement. The Africans brandished clubs, choppers, and sharpened pieces of wire. The police fired when the Africans refused to disperse. It was the most serious incident Durban has experienced in the racial crisis that is now spreading paralysis in commerce and industry in South Africa as a result of the African work boycott.[71]

The Times / News Syndication

CHAPTER 21

1962: FUTURE FATHER-IN-LAW

We were sitting together in the living room of their apartment on the second floor of a big, old house in Cleveland, Ohio, a family group: my boyfriend, Alan, his mother, father, and sister. The Christmas tree lights blinked on and off, capturing our attention. It was a bitterly cold day with a foot of snow on the ground, so we were enjoying the warmth of the sun coming in the window. The icicles hanging from the eaves melted slowly, drip, drip, dripping.

I didn't know much about Alan's family except that they were Canadians by birth. I first met his father when he came to Philadelphia and took us out to dinner at the famous Old Original Bookbinders seafood restaurant, in spite of the fact that we had told him I am allergic to seafood.

The football game was playing on the TV in the other room, where Alan went to watch the game. His father looked at his newspaper for a few minutes before going to the kitchen to fetch a beer, rejoining us in the living room. Tall, with steel grey hair, he had noticeably large hands and broad shoulders. He had starred as an Olympics-level paddler, trained by his father at the Parkdale Canoe Club in Toronto. I was instructed that you "paddle" a canoe, you do not "row" it. He reached down occasionally to share some of his beer with his English Setter, Blaze, pouring a little into a bowl beside his chair. The dog slurped at it, noisily. He picked up his discarded newspaper and tapped it against his leg, whistling through his teeth. I was taken by surprise when he turned to me and asked me about living in South Africa.

"What was it like living in South Africa? Were you and your family affected by apartheid?"

"I don't remember much about the earlier years, but there were times when there were protests and large groups of Africans would swarm into the city. That was frightening. They made an eerie high-pitched ululating sound called 'trilling' that sends shivers down your spine."

He asked if my father had disagreed with the government's policies about race. I explained that he hadn't dared to protest. He didn't want to put the church under the spotlight. The government could have closed down the church and sent us back to America. Besides, if you spoke out against apartheid, you could be put under house arrest, banned, or sent into exile. One of our friends had a boyfriend who was banned for being an activist, I explained. He wasn't allowed to meet with more than one person at a time, his house was watched, and the security police tapped his phone.

He wanted to know whether we had black servants. We did. We employed a cook, an ironing 'girl,' and a garden 'boy.' Our parents were told by the members of the white church that the Africans needed work, that it was a kindness to hire them. The women knew of servants they could recommend and advised my mother about how much to pay them. My sister Jeannette says she met a young American woman, a consul's wife, who tried to do without servants when she and her husband moved to South Africa. The trouble was, she said, people came visiting at nine o'clock in the morning so they would be out of the house while their maids were cleaning. As a result, she couldn't get her own housework done. Also, the South African women had very high standards, even the legs of the tables and chairs must gleam with polish, and cucumbers must be sliced impossibly thin. The consul's wife gave in and hired some help.

I told Mr. Longstaff that "our servants were given rooms to live in and food and uniforms to wear. Mother made sure they got medical care when they needed it and time off to go to church or visit their friends. My parents were criticized by the church members for doing things like allowing the African ministers to use the telephone in Dad's office, or for letting them sit in the front seat of the car when Mom was taking them some place like a doctor's office at the hospital."

I don't think he meant to interrogate me, but his questions were making me uncomfortable. Not many people in America had asked me about living in South Africa. I wished that Alan would come back from watching the game. I could have joined him, but I thought football games were boring. They hadn't played American football in South Africa. Instead they played rugby, soccer, and cricket, due to the British influence.

Mr. Longstaff would eventually be my father-in-law, so for me this proved to be a difficult beginning to our relationship. He cleared his throat and drummed his fingers on his knee, clamping his jaws together, a habit I later learned to interpret as a method of holding his feelings in check. He continued with his questions. "Did your family come back because of the Sharpeville Massacre?"

"What do you mean? It wasn't a massacre. The police had to defend themselves!"

"They killed people who were unarmed."

"No, no, that's not right, the Africans were rioting. There were thousands of them, threatening a small group of policeman at the police station, there were maybe just three policemen. A group of rioting Africans had recently killed some white policemen in Cato Manor in Durban so they were scared."

His tone of voice sounded accusing to me. I felt confused, affronted. I blushed as he continued with these questions, uncomfortable both physically and emotionally. I had an unfortunate ability to blush easily, all the way from my chest to the top of my forehead. When I was embarrassed or upset, or taken by surprise, I blushed. Blushing makes you feel hot and uncomfortable all by itself, let alone as the effect of a string of questions you feel you can't answer.

I didn't feel safe under his questioning. The room was overheated, the thermostat kept higher than what I was used to at home. It takes years to acclimate to stuffy, overheated American houses when you are used to the open, airy environment of houses in the tropics.

He didn't perceive my distress. I couldn't confront him. He went on, stating firmly:

"Those policemen shot unarmed women."

"They didn't mean to kill them—the crowd was growing all day and getting restless. The policemen were afraid." I could understand why they might have been scared. Mr. Longstaff brought me back to the conversation.

"They killed innocent women and children and wounded many others."

"I really don't think you have the story right. That's not what we were told."

I wished he would stop. I wonder why I didn't just walk out of the room. That would have been impolite, and I had a real fear of authority acquired from years of attending a strict British school. Durban Girls College was a private school for girls, run like a British school, almost militaristic. No talking; walk in straight lines; keep the seams of your stockings straight; don't push up your sleeves like a washerwoman; no permed hair; no pierced ears; sit up straight and keep your knees together under your desk; wear your uniform in public, including your shoes and your hat. I would not have dared to contradict my own father any more than I would have argued with the headmistress of my school, and here I was speaking against what Mr. Longstaff was saying, and I didn't really know him. I wanted to escape, turn away from the questions. It was suffocating, bewildering, the fear that he could be right? It was making me feel as though I were somehow guilty, responsible, like my not being any good at mathematics.

"Weren't they peaceful protestors?"

"They were supposed to be at work. They were striking. The police were scared. There were too many of them. They shot defensively, to protect themselves."

"I thought they were protesting the pass laws—a lot of them were women?"

"They were throwing rocks at the police."

"The police sent armored vehicles—wasn't that a rather strong reaction, sure to incite more violence?"

I brought him back to one of his first questions, whether we'd left South Africa because of Sharpeville. No, the church had already decided to bring us back because one of the pastors was ready to retire and they wanted my Dad to take his place in Philadelphia.

A loud cheering from the football game gained his attention and he left the room, carrying his beer, whistling through his teeth again. The dog padded after him, perhaps hoping for another bowl of beer. I sat there, thinking about my reaction to his words. People didn't usually ask me about living in South Africa. One of my high school friends told my classmates I had lived in a grass hut and had a little black baby I had to leave behind. I'm afraid some of them believed this mischief, a fact I discovered much later. I suppose there was some international television news, but happenings in South Africa would have been reported mostly in newspapers and news magazines. When we were in high school, we only read the paper if it was required for a current events assignment, so, in retrospect, I am not surprised at the other students' lack of knowledge. Besides the U.S. was reeling under its own civil rights problems. He never brought up the subject of South Africa again, in all the years I knew him. It was a strained beginning to our relationship, but it was an important beginning for me, as I began to think about what he had told me.

<hr />

EXTENSION OF UNIVERSITY EDUCATION ACT, ACT NO. 45 OF 1959

The Act effectively removed from South Africa's universities their freedom to admit students of their choice. It put an end to black students attending white universities, separating tertiary institutions according to race. The Bill was passed in the face of large and influential opposition from the universities and students in South Africa, and from students and academicians all over the world.

Dr. D. F. Malan proclaimed that the enforcement of University Apartheid was "urgent" state policy. The motivation for this bill is illustrated by the following:

"I am confident that no European at Winburg or anywhere else will tolerate their son or daughter sitting in the same class room with non-Europeans. This is the reason why the Government is doing everything in its power to establish black universities." (C. R. Swart, State President, then Minister of Justice, *Cape Times,* 25th March 1957.)

"We do not want (Non-Europeans) in the same university as the young European students of today, who are the leaders of tomorrow. We do not want Europeans to become so accustomed to the native that they feel there is no difference between them and the natives." (Dr. H. F. Verwoerd, Prime Minister, then Minister of Native Affairs, *Cape Argus* 19th March 1958.)

[Winston Nagan, *The New African*][72]

Chapter 22

Africa House: Northwestern University

Two years later, a student at Northwestern University, I was thrilled to discover that there was a Department of African Studies. Dr. Gwendolen Carter, referred to as "Miss Carter," was Director. Once a small residence, Africa House was a cozy place. There was just the one classroom: the remaining rooms were offices. I decided to find out what was going on there. After introducing myself and explaining my background, I was offered a part-time job. One of my assignments was to read all the newspapers that came into the department, mostly from England and South Africa. I cut out all the articles discussing South Africa and arranged them in a scrapbook for Miss Carter to read later. The papers represented different points of view. The ones I remember most clearly are the London *Times*, the Manchester *Guardian* and the Johannesburg *Star*. When living in South Africa, my family had always referred to the *Star* as a "rag." It was a perfect job for me. As I read, I learned, and it opened up a whole new point of view for me. However, I didn't arrange the clippings the way Miss Carter would have preferred and she let me know she was displeased.

I worked in a room that once had been the kitchen, with a photocopier and a big table where I could spread out the newspapers. I sometimes listened in on discussions between the graduate students and professors as they gathered after class. I wished I could attend those classes, but I was still a lowly undergraduate and not a political science major. They were talking about how the South African government had established Bantu homelands, or Bantustans, areas for Africans to live where they would purportedly govern themselves. The students said the leaders of the homelands were just puppets of the apartheid government, and the residents were required to give up all South African citizenship rights. The establishment of the black national states was one of the things that pushed the heretofore non-violent black activists to consider violence. Some of the Bantustans were physically divided into non-integral sections. One of the black homelands, the Transkei, was geographically situated just south of the province of Natal, where we had lived. Most of the residents were Xhosa-speaking. Their culture had already been disrupted by the British. Dr. Carter and another professor were writing a book on the subject.[73] I was beginning to form a more realistic understanding of apartheid—as it became even more radical in this later phase.

Dr. Carter served as a liaison to the U.S. State Department. In preparation for a trip to South Africa, she stopped in Washington, DC before flying to Johannesburg. She told us afterwards that she met someone on the steps of the University of the Witwatersrand in Johannesburg who handed her several notebooks, wrapped in brown paper. The notebooks had been buried deep in the ground for safe-keeping because they listed the names of members of the Natal Indian Congress and the Pan Africanist Congress, activist organizations that had been banned by the South African government as "Communist" organizations. The people listed in those books would be endangered if the notebooks fell into the hands of the South African secret police. Miss Carter carried them out of the country in a diplomatic bag which she delivered to the State Department before returning to Northwestern. White South Africa was becoming more and more isolated and paranoid.

The following year, my senior year as an undergraduate major in English and Linguistics, I was granted an independent study. I was introduced to a young African man who came from the area at the foot of Mount Kilimanjaro in what is now called Tanzania. His native language was KiChagga, and it was my assignment to elicit, or draw out, his spoken language and write it down, which had never been done. Our sessions were supervised by my professor, Dr. Hans Wolff, who recorded our work. I really enjoyed it and was excited about the idea of doing something similar with other cultures after graduation. That was my goal. Linguistic work like that was generally sponsored by churches and missionary groups.

While I was working there, the African Studies program received an invitation from an organization in Chicago to take part in a panel discussion on South Africa. I was invited to be one of the participants. Members of the audience initially directed their questions to me, broad questions that couldn't be answered quickly or easily, such as, "What was it like living in South Africa?" In spite of the fact that they were genuinely interested, I felt acutely uncomfortable, exposed, I was totally unprepared. I'd had no previous experience with public speaking. Sitting up on the stage with the professor and the graduate students, facing that audience, I felt that I didn't really belong there. It was as though my ignorance was being publicly unveiled. I was also keenly aware that graduate students often look down on undergraduates, and this group of students was no exception. They didn't know how to deal with me. I was only twenty years old. I've been told I was thought of as an enigma. After that experience, I decided it might be safer to tell people I grew up in Africa, as the term "South Africa" only created discomfort.

Regarding Dr. Carter: I lived in her house that summer in exchange for taking care of the lawn and her flower bed. The lawn ended up in stripes because I applied the fertilizer incorrectly and burned some areas. I pulled out the Portulaca flower seedlings, thinking they were the weeds she had carefully pointed out to me before she left on her trip to South Africa, which left the weeds to take over the flowerbed. She must have been disappointed, but she never said a word to me about it.

In 2005 I took a job as an academic librarian, a faculty position, at Saint Leo University, near Tampa. Among the many strengths of this Benedictine Catholic university is the firm belief in introducing students to the concept of social justice. One of the programs I helped coordinate, *Focus the Nation*, encouraged students to explore both social and environmental justice and to present their research to student and faculty audiences in disciplines across the curriculum. I wrote articles and presentations about topics such as genocide in Darfur, the effect of climate change on human rights, and the prostitutes of New York. This focus on social justice brought me closer to my feelings about South Africa, apartheid, and the years I had spent growing up there. It was as if I had completed the circle. It was time to try and put the experience down on paper to share with others.

⟶⟩➤●◄⟨⟵

THE TERRORISM ACT, ACT NO 83 OF 1967

Allowed for indefinite detention without trial and established BOSS, the Bureau of State Security, which was responsible for the internal security of South Africa … Provided startlingly broad definitions of "terrorism."

The wide network of political controls aimed at the maintenance of 'law and order' pales into insignificance when compared with the draconian powers of the Terrorism Act. By the enactment of this measure, the criminal code was entirely rewritten and "disappearance in the night, that dreaded phenomenon of the police state," became a reality.

"Why do Detainees Die?"
Section 6 of the Terrorism Act gives the Police complete power to detain anybody at all indefinitely and without trial. THEY DO THIS IN SECRET IF THEY SO WISH. How many people are being held in South Africa's prisons without trial? NOBODY KNOWS.

One man was held in prison for two years. Nobody knew—until he appeared in court at the end of that period.

The Wilcox brother and sister were detained in February, 1971. They [have] just been released after nine lost months—WITHOUT being charged with any offence; WITHOUT explanation; WITHOUT apology; WITH- OUT compensation.

Mrs. Timol: "When can I see my son again?"

Police: "You won't see your son again."

[*Black Sash News*][74]

CONCLUSION

A minority regime which can only be maintained through violence has forfeited its right to exist because it is unjust in conception and application.[75]

Breyten Breytenbach, *The Namibian*

After we returned to America in 1960, the civil rights struggle of the 1960s and '70s were followed by a wave of anti-apartheid sentiment and calls for divestment in South Africa by American college students. But economic sanctions against the regime were not applied by the U.S. government until the mid-1980s. At that time, I worried that increased economic hardship might harm the people who had lived so close to us, the very people the sanctions were supposed to help. The growing spotlight on apartheid bred widespread contempt for white South Africans, who suffered attribution as oppressors no matter who they were. The African political leadership was becoming more vociferous, especially the African National Congress—I feared that their growing power would result in violence against our Zulu friends, most of whom belonged to the traditionally ethnic political group, Inkatha. The ANC believed Inkatha was giving in to the government's demands too easily.

This was the beginning of a conflicted period in my life. Once I had started asking myself the question, "What is the truth?" then layer after layer of non-truth had to be peeled off.

Apartheid was a separation imposed upon the majority who populated that beautiful land but who were designated by government Act to live out their lives as a subordinate class of people, considered not worthy of the white man's privilege. It was a division determined by politics and race, influenced by religion. Like other white people who lived in South Africa in those days, I've carried both guilt and shame for being an unaware, unwilling participant. I have taken to heart the severe but thoughtful criticism of black South Africans who feel only scorn for those of us with the temerity to mention our guilt as if we were to be pitied. I have questioned my parents' belief in protecting us from the truth; and I have wondered how far a child is capable of processing the idea of bigotry.

I returned to South Africa with my husband, Alan Longstaff, in the early 1990s. The church sent us to prepare for a conference to take place the following year. Alan was also asked to work with the African ministers on practical matters such as finances and budgets. He reported to the church administration in America that the budget for the African church should be increased; also, he stressed that they should have representation on the church's governing bodies. This positive new approach to the needs of the African church coincided with the immense changes in South African government that occurred after Mandela was elected president and the machinery of the apartheid regime was dismantled. A white, mostly male church administration found itself dealing with the "new" South Africa, which proved to be both exciting and frustrating, depending on your point of view. I once argued with a church official who, pointing to the nicely dressed women in a video I had taken at the conference, said, "She is well-dressed. It doesn't look like she needs a lot of financial support." The clothes were castoffs that had belonged to the woman's mistress. She was the maid. After decades of difficulties, the search for solutions has now resulted in a quality of respect toward African church officials that was hard to find in previous years.

It was my editor who suggested that I expand the pages at the end of each chapter to show how the Acts of Apartheid affected people outside our family, thereby giving substance to the "shadow" I was talking about. My initial research ended in frustration—it was difficult to find the material I needed. Australian and British newspapers seemed to be the best source of articles on apartheid in the 1950s, since South Africa was a Commonwealth state within the British Empire until 1961, when it became the Republic of South Africa. But it was thanks to a South African librarian, Dr. Archie Dick, University of Pretoria, that I discovered the vast resources of *Digital Innovation South Africa*, based at the University of KwaZulu Natal. There I was able to research multiple South African news sources, most of them small, liberal presses, many of them eventually banned by the apartheid government.

I had never realized the full extent of the strangulating hold the apartheid government had over the English language press. It is a fascinating tale of persistence in the face of anything the government could think of to stop the truth from coming out. Those journalists never gave up the fight for freedom of expression.

One of the articles that particularly struck me was the report by the South African Council of Churches, *Apartheid and the Church* (see an excerpt following Chapter 6). The report listed all the rules and restrictions on churches, foreign religious organizations included. I had read an article questioning the moral right of the clergy who had not stood up to apartheid,[76] so this report clarified for me just what my father faced in staying the course. Outspoken clergy were arrested, interrogated, imprisoned, banned, and exiled. I can't blame my father for wanting to avoid this fate: it would have ended his service to our church in South Africa and endangered both his own family and the Africans he supervised.

I could not possibly cover the whole story here, but I hope that what I have provided will increase the reader's understanding. This was a journey I never expected to take, but learning the details of the inhumanity of apartheid has removed remaining layers of confusion and brought me to a place where I can let the happy memories remain just where they are, stories brought from far away. As for what was living in those shadows—there is a sad truth, if no comfort, in the words of Nelson Mandela, the first black president of South Africa:

After climbing a great hill, one only finds that there are many more hills to climb.[77]

APPENDIX

THE COLOURED PEOPLE OF SOUTH AFRICA

According to the Population Registration Act of 1950, South Africans were divided into four distinct categories: Whites, Indians, African and Coloureds. The Coloured group was further subdivided into "Cape Malay," Khoisan, and other Coloureds. Researchers have pointed out that the Coloured identity has never been seen as an identity in its own right because it has been negatively defined and did not fit the classificatory schemes created by the apartheid politicians.

The Coloured people of South Africa were the product of liaisons between white, European men and local indigenous female inhabitants, the Khoisan. Khoisan is a term used by physical anthropologists to distinguish the aboriginal people of southern Africa from their black African farming neighbors.[78]

Europeans first appeared at the Cape when the Dutch established a supply and trading post there in 1652. The Dutch East India Company, under Jan van Riebeeck, sought to establish a sea route to India with the intention of expanding their participation in the valuable spice trade.

Enslaved peoples were brought to South Africa by the Dutch East India Company. They became known as the "Cape Malay," and were mainly Muslim political exiles from Indonesia. West Africans from slave ships captured at sea were another source of slaves. A distinctive culture arose among these people, whose DNA now shows a wide variety of ethnicities.

The Afrikaans language evolved as a language of its own through a simplification of Dutch in order for the slaves to be able to communicate with the Dutch and amongst each other. Educated Muslims were the first to write texts in Afrikaans. The "Cape Malay" community generally speak mostly Afrikaans.[79]

Note: Prime Minister Verwoerd was assassinated on September 6, 1966 by Dimitri Tsafendas, a young Coloured man whose mother was African and his father Greek.

THE BLACK SASH

A number of articles are attributed to the Black Sash. I can remember seeing these indomitable women standing on the steps in front of the Durban City Hall, with a wide black sash across one shoulder, crossing over their chests down to their waists. The Black Sash remains a strong organization dedicated to the belief that human rights are not a privilege, but include the rights of all, "those in the dawn of life, the dusk of life, or the shadows of life" [Kay Grainger]

"The conscience of white South Africa": Celebrating the Black Sash, 60 years later

Started in 1955 over a cup of tea by six middle-class white women outraged by the then-government's attempts at removing "Coloured" citizens from the voter's roll, the Black Sash developed into a powerful force for protest and change and served as a visible prod to the consciences of those who implemented and benefited from an unjust system.

The women relentlessly campaigned and mobilized, first against the legal amendment—a battle they lost—and then later against almost every other violation of human rights by the Apartheid state including racial segregation, migrant labour, influx control, detention without trial, state censorship, and the various states of emergency the government imposed on the country.

The Black Sash were also an invaluable source of information for newspapers operating in difficult circumstances with constant harassment by the state, bringing vital news to the attention of journalists.

The Sash kept up the pressure throughout the increasingly violent 1960s, campaigning against the government's plans to set up "homelands" and forcibly remove South Africans to these areas and also staged campaigns, sit-ins and vigils after the Sharpeville Massacre in 1960.

The women of the Sash continued to offer support or to use their position as mostly privileged white women to highlight events locally and internationally.

Marianne Hamm, 14 May, 2015

www.blacksash.org.za

NOTES

[1] Nancy Napier, *Spiritual Memoir.*

[2] See J.R.R. Tolkien, *The Lord of the Rings* (New York: Houghton Mifflin, 1992): 64.

[3] Aminatta Forna, 2002, 18.

Chapter 1: The Population Registration Act

[4] Owen Williams, "The Village and the Castle," *Africa South* 3, no. 1 (Oct-Dec 1958): 26-27. Digital Innovation South Africa.

[5] "Pass Laws: Southern Transvaal States the Facts," *The Black Sash* 4, no. 4 (Aug 1960): 14-16. Digital Innovation South Africa.

[6] The Black Sash. "Memorandum on the Pass Laws and Influx Control." *Reality* 6, no. 4, Introduction, Revised (Sept 1974): 19. Digital Innovation South Africa.

Chapter 2: The Reservation of Separate Amenities Act

[7] Leonard Thompson 2001, p201

[8] J. Nieuwenhuysen, "Selfless, Committed Doctor Kept the Faith for Freedom and Equity," *The Age,* Obituaries (Melbourne, Australia), (Nov 25 2013): 38.

[9] H.F. Verwoerd, "Speech by Prime Minister Dr. H.F. Verwoerd on the Fifth Anniversary of The Republic," Monument Hill, Pretoria, May 31, 1966. www.boerevryheid.co.za/

Chapter 3: The Group Areas Act

[10] Yusuf Cachalia, "The Ghetto Act," *Africa South* 2, no. 1 (Sept-Oct 1957): 39. Digital Innovation South Africa.

[11] Myrna Blumberg, "Durban Explodes: Riots, Demonstrations, Violence," *Africa South* 4, no. 1 (Oct-Dec 1959): 13-14. Digital Innovation South Africa.

[12] "Widows Must Leave Their Homes: City Council Refuses to Budge," *New Age* (Northern Edition) 9, no. 7 (Thurs Nov 29, 1962): 6. Digital Innovation South Africa.

[13] "Just Put Them in a Home," *Liberal Opinion* 1, no 3 (March 1962): 4. Digital Innovation South Africa.

Chapter 4: The Defiance Campaign of 1952

[14] "Defiance Campaign in South Africa, Recalled," The O'Malley Archives, The Nelson Mandela Foundation.

[15] "African Defiance Campaign Extends to Natal," *Inverell Times* (NSW) (Mon 1Sep 1952): 1.

[16] "The Public Safety Act," Omics International. *www.research.omicsgroup.org/index.php/Public_Safety_Act,_1953.* (Creative Commons)

[17] J.C. Greyling, as quoted in "The Press: Strijdom's 'Last Barrier' by George Clay and Stanley Uys. *Africa South* 2, No. 1 (Oct-Dec 1957): 29. Digital Innovation South Africa.

Chapter 5: The Abolition of Passes and Coordination of Documents Act

[18] W.B. Ngakane, *The Black Sash* 2, no. 9 (Nov 1957): 5-6. Digital Innovation South Africa.

[19] Dan Tloome. *Interview with Dan Tloome by Julie Frederickse*, p2 (undated). Digital Innovation South Africa.

Chapter 6: Apartheid and the Church

[20] Rose, 2013.

[21] Basutoland, now the Kingdom of Lesotho, is completely surrounded by South Africa. In the 1950s the country was under the protection of the British. It was granted independence in October, 1966.

[22] Peter Randall, Gen. Ed., "Apartheid and the Church: Report of the Church Commission of the Study Project on Christianity in Apartheid Society regarding the effects of apartheid on the Church in South Africa," (Johannesburg, 1972). Digital Innovation South Africa

Chapter 7: The Bantu Education Act

23 Baard, Frances and Barbie Schreiner, *My Spirit is Not Banned* (Harare: Zimbabwe Publishing House, 1986). Accessed at South African History Online. www.sahistory.org.za

24 Duma Nokwe, "The Meaning of Bantu Education," *Liberation* 9 (1954):12-18. Digital Innovation South Africa.

Chapter 8: The Separate Representation of Voters Act

25 Helen Joseph. *Tomorrow's Sun* (New York: The John Day Co., 1967): 69-70.

26 Uys Krige, "Our Coloured People," Address given in Cape Town at a Public Protest Meeting called by the Black Sash against Proclamation 26—Apartheid in Entertainment and Sport, *The Black Sash* 9: no. 3 (Aug 1965): 19, 21.

Chapter 9: Women Hold up Half the Sky

27 *www.wimbledon.com/en_GB/atoz/clothing_and_equipment.html*

28 *Women Hold up Half the Sky*, South African History Archive, SAHA exhibition for Women's Month 2016. www.saha.org.za. Accessed May 30, 2017. Reproduced with permission.

29 Helen Joseph, "What Does it Mean to a Woman to Carry a Pass," *Africa South* 2, no. 2 (Jan-Mar 1958): 26, 29, 31. Digital Innovation South Africa.

30 Dennis Kiley, "The Pondoland Massacre," *Africa South* 5, no. 1 (Oct-Dec 1960): 8. Digital Innovation South Africa.

Chapter 10: The Prohibition of Mixed Marriages Act

31 Peter Randall, 1972. "Apartheid and the Church," p13. Digital Innovation South Africa.

32 Julius Lewin, "Sex, Colour and the Law" *Africa South* 4, no. 3 (Apr-Jun 1960): 68. Digital Innovation South Africa.

33 Muriel Horrell, "Legislation and race relations: A summary of the main South African laws which affect race relationships," Rev. Ed. (Johannesburg: South African Institute of Race Relations, 1971): 13. Digital Innovation South Africa.

Chapter 11: The Suppression of Communism Act

[34] South African History Online, [online], Available at www.sahistory.org.za

[35] Jean Sinclair, "South Africa in Crisis," *The Black Sash* 8: no. 3 (Oct/Nov 1964): 4. Digital Innovation South Africa.

[36] Franz Erasmus, as quoted in "The Press: Strijdom's Last Barrier," *Africa South* 2, no. 1 (Oct-Dec 1957). Digital Innovation South Africa.

[37] Benjamin Pogrund, *War of Words: Memoirs of a South African Journalist.* (New York: Seven Stories Press, 2000): 166.

[38] Riotous Assemblies and Suppression of Communism Act. www.africanhistory.about.com/od/apartheidlaws/g/No15of54.htm

[39] "Banning," *New Age* (Northern Edition) 9, no. 7 (Thurs Nov 29, 1962): 5. Digital Innovation South Africa.

Chapter 12: The Bantu Authorities Act

[40] Benjamin Pogrund, "Report on a Trip to Rural areas of the Transvaal, *War of Words: Memoirs of a South African Journalist* (New York: Seven Stories Press, 2000): 136.

Chapter 13: The Natives Resettlement Act

[41] "Sophiatown," South African History Online, [online], Available at www.sahistory.org.za

[42] Lawrence Morgan, "The Strategies of Bantu Resettlement," *Black Sash News,* 13, no. 4 (Feb 1970): 15. Digital Innovation South Africa.

[43] "Black Spots," *Liberal Opinion* (Jul 1962): 4. South African History Online, [online], Available at www.sahistory.org.za

[44] David Hemson, "Removals," *Reality* 4, no. 4 (Sept 1972): 15. Digital Innovation South Africa.

Chapter 14: The Native Urban Areas Amendment Act

[45] Elliott, 1953.

[46] Muriel Horrell, *Legislation and Race Relations: A Summary of the main South African laws which affect race relationships.* South African Institute of Race Relations, Rev. Ed. Native Laws Amendment Act of 1952, 4 [Johannesburg, 1971]: 36. Digital Innovation South Africa.

[47] "Native Urban Areas Amendment Act," O'Malley Archives. The Nelson Mandela Foundation

[48] Marian Lacy, "Zanyokwe—For Betterment or Worse?" *The Black Sash/Die Swart Serp* 21, no. 4 (Feb. 1980): 23. Digital Innovation South Africa.

Chapter 15: The Defence Act

[49] Gilbert Marcus, "The Gagging Writs," *Reality,* 19, no. 3 (May 1987): 8-9. Digital Innovation South Africa.

[50] Bryan Trabold. "Hiding Our Snickers: *Weekly Mail* Journalists' Indirect Resistance in Apartheid South Africa," *College English* 68, no. 4 (Mar. 2006): 382-406. Copyright 2006 by the National Council of Teachers of English. Used with permission.

[51] Nadine Gordimer, in "Censorship and the Primary Homeland," *Reality* (Jan 1970): 12. Digital Innovation South Africa.

[52] Hallett, Robin, "Understanding Black Africa," The Maurice Webb Memorial Lecture 1972, published in *Reality: A Journal of Liberal and Radical Opinion* 4, no. 6 (Jan 1973) p5. Accessed online at www.patontrust.co.za April 3, 2017. Digital Information South Africa.

[53] Subry Govander, "Writing in a time of Racism: The South African Media in the 70s." This story first appeared on *The Journalist* www.thejournalist.org.za/

Chapter 16: The Native Laws Amendment Act of 1957

[54] Alan Paton, "Association by Permission," *Africa South* 1, no. 4 (Jul-Sept 1957): 14. Digital Innovation South Africa.

[55] "Funerals," *Reality* 19, no. 3 (May 1987): 9. Digital Innovation South Africa.

Chapter 17: The Soweto Schools Uprising

[56] Bunting, 1964, [6].

[57] Mary Benson, *The Sun Will Rise: Statements from the Dock by Southern African Political Prisoners* (London. 15 Jul 1981), Introduction. anc.org.za

[58] Winnie Mandela, "Interview with Winnie Mandela," by Eric Abraham. Wits Historical Papers, June 18, 1976. Digital Innovation South Africa.

Chapter 18: The Ghetto Act

[59] Mahatma Gandhi, *The Story of My Experiments with Truth*, 1927. www.un.org/events/nonviolence/2008/ International Day of Non-Violence, 2 October, 2008

[60] "The Ghetto Act," Yusuf Cachalia, *Africa South* 2, no. 1 (Oct-Dec, 1957): 39. Digital Information South Africa.

[61] "GENOCIDE!" *New Age* 6, no. 16 (Thurs, February 4, 1960): 3. Digital Information South Africa.

Chapter 19: The General Laws Amendment Act 1962

[62] "General Laws Amendment Act." South African History Online. www.sahistory.org.za

[63] Hon. O.D. Schreiner, "House Arrest and the Rule of Law," *The Star,* republished in *The Black Sash/Die Swart Serp (Dec 1962/Jan 1963)*. Digital Innovation South Africa.

[64] Helen Joseph. *Tomorrow's Sun: A Smuggled Journal from South Africa.* (New York: The John Day Co., 1967): 224.

[65] "Helen Joseph," South African History Online [online], available at www.sahistory.org.za/people/helen-joseph

[66] "Mass Protests by University Staffs in Natal," *The Times* (Jul 1, 1963): 8. The Times / News Syndication

[67] "Chronology of Apartheid Legislations" from *South African History Online,* [online], Available at www.sahistory.org.za Accessed June 8, 2017.

Chapter 20: The Sharpeville Massacre; State of Emergency

[68] Joe Gqabi, "Mass Slaughter by Police," *New Age* (Northern Ed.), 6, no. 23 (Johannesburg. Thurs Mar 24, 1960). Digital Innovation South Africa.

[69] Peter Goodspeed, "Vilified Apartheid-era Minister Dies a Hero: Denounced segregation. Sharpeville was Beyers Naude's Crisis of Faith," *National Post,* (The Financial Post) (Canada), National Edition. WORLD section (Weds, Sept 8, 2004): A11.

[70] Alan Rake, "A State of Emergency," *Africa South* 5, no. 1 (Oct-Dec 1960):14. Digital Innovation South Africa.

[71] *The Times,* "State of Emergency Extended to 31 More Districts," (April 2 1960): 6. The Times / News Syndication

Chapter 21: The Extension of University Education Act

[72] Winston Nagan, "Extension of University Education Act," *The New African* (Jul 1965): 101. Digital Information South Africa.

Chapter 22: The Terrorism Act

[73] Gwendolen M. Carter, Thomas Karis, and Newell M. Stultz. *South Africa's Transkei: the politics of domestic colonialism.* (Evanston, Ill: Northwestern University Press, 1967).

[74] "The Terrorism Act," *Black Sash News* 15, no. 3 (Dec 1971): 2-3. Digital Innovation South Africa.

Conclusion

[75] Breyten Breytenbach, upon receiving the Rapport Prize for Literature in Pretoria. *The Namibian,* (April 18, 1986): 7.

[76] David R. Penna, review of *Facing the Truth: South African Faith Communities and the Truth and Reconciliation Commission,* by James Cochrane, John de Gruchy and Stephen Martin, eds. *African Studies Quarterly* 4 (Fall 2000): 77–80.

[77] Mandela 1994, p544.

[78] www.southafrica.net/za/en/articles/entry/article-southafrica.net-the-khoisan-people

[79] *South African History Online.* www.sahistory.org.za/article/cape-malay

BIBLIOGRAPHY

SOURCES CITED

African National Congress: South Africa's National Liberation Movement *www.anc.org.za*

Bunting, Brian. *The Rise of the South African Reich.* (Penguin Africa Library, 1964, 1969). Accessed April 4, 2017 as reproduced in The O'Malley Archives, The Nelson Mandela Foundation.

Elliot, Geraldine. *The Long Grass Whispers.* (London: Routledge & Kegan Paul, 1939, 1953).

Forna, Aminatta. *The Devil that Danced on the Water: A Daughter's Quest.* (NY: Grove Press, 2002).

Joseph, Helen. *Tomorrow's Sun: A Smuggled Journal from South Africa.* (NY: The John Day Co., 1967).

Mandela, Nelson. *Long Walk to Freedom: The Autobiography of Nelson Mandela.* (NY: Little, Brown and Company, 1994).

Napier, Nancy. *Spiritual memoir,* (n.d) *www.spiritualmemoir.com/spiritual-memoir/quotations/*

Progrund, Benjamin. *War of Words: Memoir of a South African Journalist,* 1st ed. (NY: Seven Stories Press; 2000).

Rose, Jonathan Searle. *Who was Swedenborg, What Shall I Read?* YouTube video, 8:00 (Swedenborg Foundation, Westchester, PA: June 7, 2013). *www.youtube.com/watch?v=HEa0e8AcS78*

Thompson, Leonard. *A History of South Africa.* 3rd ed. (New Haven: Yale University Press, 2000).

Sources Consulted

Clark, Nancy L. & E. Alpers, *Africa and the West: From Colonialism to Independence, 1875 to the present.* (Oxford University Press, 2010).

Dick, Archie Leonard. "Librarians and crises in the 'old' and 'new' South Africa," *IFLA Journal* (May, 2016) 42: 2, 102–108.

Frank, Welsh. *A History of South Africa* (London: HarperCollins, 2000).

Guelke, Adrian. *Rethinking the Rise and Fall of Apartheid: South Africa and World Politics.* Rethinking World Politics (NY: Palgrave Macmillan, 2005).

Jackson, Gordon. *Breaking Story: The South Africa Press*, 1st ed. (Boulder: Westview Press; 1993).

Pearse, R.O. *Barrier of Spears: Drama of the Drakensberg.* (Cape Town: Howard Timmins, 1973).

Penna, David R. *Justice and Morality in South Africa.* Review of *Facing the Truth: South African Faith Communities and the Truth and Reconciliation Commission,* by James Cochrane, John de Gruchy and Stephen Martin, eds. *African Studies Quarterly* 4 (Fall 2000): 77–80.

Sparks, Allister. *The Mind of South Africa.* (New York: Ballantine Books, 1990).

Van Woerden, Henk. *The Assassin: A Story of Race and Rage in the Land of Apartheid,* transl. by Dan Jacobson (New York: Henry Holt, 1998).

Worden, Nigel. *The Making of Modern South Africa: Conquest, Segregation and Apartheid.* 3rd ed. Historical Association Studies. (Oxford & Malden, Mass.: Blackwell Publishers, 2000).

WEB SOURCES

Digital Innovation South Africa, *www.disa.ukzn.ac.za*

Mahatma Gandhi in South Africa, *www.gandhi.southafrica.net/*

Nancy Napier. Spiritual Memoir, *www.spiritualmemoir.com/spiritu-al-memoir/quotations/*

Padraig O'Malley, The Nelson Mandela Centre of Memory, O'Malley Archive, *www.nelsonmandela.org/omalley/*

South African History Archive, *www.aha.org.za*

South African History Online, *www.sahistory.org.za/*

CPSIA information can be obtained
at www.ICGtesting.com
Printed in the USA
LVHW081743081118
596433LV00031B/965/P

9 781683 150114